PUBLIC REVENUE
WITHOUT TAXATION

Previous Publications

ENQUIRY INTO PRICES AND INCOMES (1968)

LOCAL GOVERNMENT FINANCE (1970)

FANFARE TO ACTION: INCOME DISTRIBUTION
AS A CAUSE OF INFLATION (1973)

SOCIAL JUSTICE OR UNBRIDLED GOVERNMENT (1976)

THE CHANCE TO CHANGE (1977)

FULL EMPLOYMENT AND PUBLIC SPENDING (1978)

PUBLIC REVENUE WITHOUT TAXATION

Ronald Burgess

SHEPHEARD-WALWYN (PUBLISHERS) LTD

First published in 1993 by
Shepheard-Walwyn (Publishers) Ltd
26 Charing Cross Road (Suite 34)
London WC2H 0DH

British Library Cataloguing in Publication Data

Burgess, Ronald
  Public Revenue Without Taxation
  I. Title
  336.2

  ISBN 0 856 83135 2

Typeset by Alacrity Phototypesetters
Banwell Castle, Weston-super-Mare
Printed and bound in Great Britain by
BPCC Wheatons Ltd, Exeter

Contents

Acknowledgements

The author wishes to acknowledge his indebtedness to the late Colin Clark who, as Director of the Agricultural Economics Research Institute at the University of Oxford, personally provided the necessary impetus for this line of research. The author also wishes to thank all members of the Economic Study Association whose invaluable support has brought this work to publication.

1
Introduction

Through this century of passing economic fashion the domi-
nating idea has swung from 'Supply creates its own Demand'
to the opposite 'Demand creates its own Supply' then back to
'Supply creates its own Demand'. The process continues;
there are signs of the pendulum beginning yet another
journey. This alternation of the dominant idea has arisen
from a division between demand-side and supply-side
theory, each enshrined in its own school of thought and each
claiming to be complete in itself. These schools describe one-
sided views which distort what is in reality a coherent
whole. Half a loaf is said to be better than no bread,
but this division of economic theory gives to each faction
only, as it were, half a pair of trousers. Such an incomplete
conceptual garment is worse than nothing. In the sphere of
government, policy prescriptions derived from half a theory
mislead both politicians and their electors. Throughout the
world governments have been misled into pursuing policies
which have led from a slump to an inflation and on to a
combination of the two — 'slumpflation'. The toast given by
Lord Keynes a few months before his death in 1946 to 'the
Royal Economic Society, economics and economists who
are the trustees, not of civilisation but of the possibility of
civilisation',[1] offers little cheer to governments and their
electors today.

The so-called Keynesian school of economic thought is
more accurately described as the demand-side school, for it
concentrates on aggregate demand and ignores the spirit and

1

much of the economics of Keynes. Its policy prescriptions seek, largely by means of a high volume of public spending, to hold aggregate demand at a level sufficient to keep an economy operating at, or close to, 'full employment'. The demand-side concept of full employment, as well as the means of sustaining it, owes more to Beveridge than Keynes. In *Full Employment in a Free Society* Beveridge wrote; 'The first condition of full employment is that the total outlay should always be high enough to set up a demand for the products of industry which cannot be satisfied without using the whole manpower of the country; only so can the number of vacant jobs be always as high, or higher, than the number looking for jobs'. For Keynes the term 'full employment' did not relate to any particular rate of unemployment but was an alternative term for what he considered to be 'a condition which might be appropriately designated as one of true inflation'.[2] Again, although Keynes did argue against the then fashionable interpretation of Say's law that supply always calls forth its own demand, he did not argue the opposite — that demand will always call forth its own supply. It is this latter non-Keynes view which appears to be the assumption underlying the demand-side school's policy prescriptions. The high level of public spending necessitated by the pursuit of 'full employment' and the large tax take, topped up by an annual public borrowing requirement needed to support this spending, proved to be a sure recipe for accelerating inflation.

In *The Economic Journal* of December 1945 Colin Clark first argued his case, on the basis of pre-World War II evidence from many countries, that inflation becomes inevitable when total general government tax revenue plus borrowing requirement exceeds 25 per cent of net national product at market prices. Lord Keynes is on record as having agreed with Clark and subsequent experience in most countries of the world would seem to support their view. The level of public spending required by demand-side full employment budget results in Clark's limit being substantially exceeded. The demand-side school's solution to the inflationary consequences of their full employment policies is the imposition of central planning to include extensive and detailed public controls over such private matters as incomes, prices, external trade and capital movements. The mal-distribution of resources and the loss of personal liberty necessitated by this remedy has so far proved unacceptable to the free electorates of the western world. This being so and with inflation rampant, the demand-side school lost its domination.

With the failing fortunes of the demand-side school the Chicago, monetarist or supply-side school of economic thought rose to become the established orthodoxy. Their first objective is the eradication of inflation. Supply-side policy prescriptions include squeezing inflation out of the system by controlling the money supply, reducing the size of the public sector by privatisation or other means, and cutting public expenditure together with the tax take. Coinciding with the implementation of these policies the rate of inflation has tended to fall world-wide but the price appears to be a return to a high level of unemployment. Professor Harry Johnson, an early adherent of the Chicago school, warned of this possibility in 1971 when he wrote, '... the Keynesians are right in their view that inflation is a far less serious problem than mass unemployment. Either we will vanquish inflation at relatively little cost, or we will get used to it'.[3] Further, where active steps have been taken to reduce the size of the public sector by privatisation, in most cases Lord Stockton's castigation of Mrs Thatcher's administration for 'selling off the family silver' seems apposite. No economic principle is apparent. When the government estimate there to be a short-term financial gain by hiving off from the public sector a particular firm or industry, then that firm or industry is sold off to the private sector. There is little or no evidence to suggest supply-side policies have been effective in reducing either public spending or the tax take. Some items of public spending may be cut but spending on other items rises. Similarly while some taxes may be cut others are increased, often by more than enough to compensate in terms of total tax revenue. In the United Kingdom the new supply-side policies are presumed to have been implemented from 1979; in that year tax revenue appropriated 38.6 per cent of net national product at market prices. A decade later tax revenue was appropriating about 40 per cent of net national product at market prices.

While the supply-side school has contributed much to the advancement of economic science, its public appeal relies on little more than a reaction to the profligate proposals of the demand-side school. It offers more freedom, less government and less taxation but also, of necessity, less public spending. The first three enjoy public support but not the last. Supply-side policies can only offer a partial remedy as they do not offer an alternative to the imposition of taxation for the purpose of defraying necessary public expenditure. Its philosophy is fundamentally flawed. For example, Nozick argues that taxation is wrong, but then proceeds to admit to its necessity.[4] He rejects outright the concept of the 'Robin Hood' principle of redistributive taxation. For such purposes, he asserts, taxation cannot be justified. Against this he recognises that governments have a duty to protect private property, defend the state and uphold law and order and for these purposes concludes the imposition of taxation to be justified. This argument could be applied equally to justify a mobster's demand for protection money. If taxation is wrong then it cannot be justified by necessity. 'Necessity', said William Pitt in 1783, 'is the plea for every infringement of human freedom. It is the argument of tyrants; it is the creed of slaves'.

For the people of the industrialised trading economies it is a fact of unfortunate experience that the policy prescriptions of the succession of orthodox established schools of economic thought have offered little more than a trade-off between unemployment and inflation — both with their accompanying social evils. When, on the advice of economists, attempts have been made to reduce unemployment by increasing public spending, then inflation has become rampant with all its accompanying evils. When effective counter-inflationary policies have been pursued, then the rate of unemployment has risen with all its accompanying evils. Some economists appear to place the blame on the politicians but this is an evasion of responsibility on the part of those very economists.[5] In matters of public economic policy politicians and governments regularly seek, and usually act upon, the advice of those claiming to expertise in the sphere of economics. One has to conclude that it is the economists who have failed.

The present dispute between the demand-side and supply-side schools of economic thought is largely irrelevant to the issue of eradicating both inflation and unemployment. It is totally irrelevant to the issue of creating a just society or even a 'property owning democracy'. In this work it will be argued that a modern trading economy can provide the setting for a just society, free of home-bred inflation and unemployment; but the first requirement is for government to stop persistently flouting the principle of private property by the imposition of taxation. Adam Smith railed against public profligacy, as do contemporary supply-siders, but he endorsed the imposition of taxation. In the *Wealth of Nations* he laid down the 'Canons of Taxation', but he accepted also that, in the absence of a fund peculiarly belonging to the public authority, then the 'necessary expenses of government' must be defrayed 'from the revenue of the people'.[6] With few exceptions later writers on public finance have followed only one of Adam Smith's leads by limiting their investigations as to what necessary public spending consists of and to the most efficient or acceptable methods of raising the required tax revenue from 'the revenue of the people'.

The supply-side school, like Adam Smith, rails against public profligacy but considers for certain purposes the imposition of taxation to be justified by necessity. The demand-side ·school considers taxation to be an essential instrument of both fiscal and social policy. Contemporary schools of economic thought must cut loose from this traditional approach if the social and economic difficulties facing trading economies are to be remedied. Economics is required to follow up Adam Smith's other lead, to which Alfred Marshall contributes with his distinction between the public and private value of freeholds, and investigate the possibilty of a source of revenue that is peculiarly public. This investigation was begun prior to Adam Smith by the Physiocrats and has been continued by the American Henry George and his followers.[7] What governments need to know from economics is a source of public revenue that arises from the very nature of a trading economy and does not offend against the principle of private property. This public revenue must be sufficient to cover necessary public expenses after the abolition of all taxation. When economists can provide this knowledge then truly they may be considered as 'trustees ... of the possibility of civilisation'.

1. R.F. Harrod, *The Life of John Maynard Keynes*.
2. J.M. Keynes, *The General Theory of Employment Interest and Money*, Bk. V, Ch.21, p.303.
3. H.G. Johnson, *The Keynesian Revolution and the Monetarist Counter-Revolution*, p.200.
4. R. Nozick, *Anarchy, State and Utopia*.
5. Colin Clark, *Taxmanship*, Institute of Economic Affairs Hobart Paper No. 26.
6. Adam Smith, *The Wealth of Nations*, Bk. V, Ch.II.
7. Henry George, *Progress and Poverty*.

2
The Failure of Economics

Taxation is, as will be argued in the following chapters of this work, a primal cause of both inflation and unemployment. The development of Keynes' general theory of employment leads to the conclusion that an open trading economy is likely to be most competitive, and therefore most prosperous, only when all taxation is abolished. Taxation raises the value of Z for all values of N (p. 20), thus in a free market a prerequisite for efficiency and competition working together to reduce an economy's aggregate supply price to a minimum is the abolition of taxation. Regardless of this, the freely elected governments of contemporary trading economies — with the acquiescence of their electorates — persist in raising the major part, if not all, of their revenues by means of taxation. The immediate cause of such action by governments, and for the acquiesence of their electorates, is ignorance of any acceptable alternative method of raising sufficient public revenue. Ignorance of any alternative has led, without any further questioning, to taxation being accepted as the necessary source of public revenue. As a consequence economic debate on public revenue has become limited to considerations of appropriate methods of raising that taxation and of the amount that might be raised. Any discussion on the possibility of an alternative source of public revenue other than taxation has vanished from orthodox economic literature. The underlying cause is, however, a failure by economists to perceive the special nature of a developed trading economy. Econo-

7

mists must, as a first step, re-investigate the basic economic processes common to all developed trading economies.

The Primary Division

In any productive process, a process by which the natural world is modified so that the human race may live and live more fully, human labour is a necessary factor. 'No work — no product' is a fundamental law of the universe. Individuals may violate this law but collectively the human race cannot. Justice works. When justice is ignored at the individual level then it works on the mass and is often described as injustice. In addition to human labour every productive process needs also one or more non-human factors. Some writers on economics lump all non-human factors together and call them 'capital'. Other writers distinguish between non-human factors in their natural state unmodified by labour, which they often call 'land', and reserve the term 'capital' for those non-human factors which have been already modified to some extent by labour. When this latter distinction is made then both land and labour are necessary factors of production and for some productive processes may be, in particular combinations, sufficient. For certain analytical purposes even finer distinctions may be useful but such distinctions do not alter the basic requirement that in any productive process a human factor plus one or more non-human factors are necessary. This holds for the most primitive productive process in a self-sufficient household as well as for the most technologically advanced process in a highly developed trading economy. There are, however, fundamental differences in the nature of a non-trading economy and a trading economy.

In a non-trading economy a productive unit such as a self-sufficient household produces an output in its entirety solely for the enjoyment and consumption of its own members. What matters to the members is the quantity and quality of the output they have laboured to produce. A bumper harvest means a year of good living whereas a poor harvest may mean death through starvation. Although such extremes of self-sufficiency may be rare today, there are many examples of communities in which individual households are the productive unit producing an output primarily for their own enjoyment and consumption, trading at most only what happens to be surplus to their needs. For them the quality and quantity of the output is of major importance and relative prices hardly matter. On the other hand in a trading economy an output is produced primarily for sale. In this fundamentally different circumstance what matters to a productive enterprise is not only the quality and quantity of the output but also the per unit market prices of that output. For example, if a bumper harvest leads to depressed market prices, then farmers may suffer, while the enhanced prices following upon a poor harvest may work to their benefit. Thus in a trading economy the emphasis is on income rather than output, and an important factor determining the nominal income of a productive enterprise is market prices.

For a non-trading economy comprising self-sufficient productive units Ricardo's theory of rent is directly applicable. The same capital and labour applied to the least fertile land in use will produce less output than when applied to the most fertile land in use. In Ricardian terms this difference in output is 'rent' and it arises solely from the differences in the fertility of the soil in use at a particular location over that at the margin of cultivation. Given private ownership of land the primary division of the output is between rent, the share of the output accruing to the landowners, and wages, the share of the output accruing to those who supplied the labour. The return to capital is a secondary claim on wages. In the case of a trading economy Ricardo's theory of rent is not directly applicable. In general differences in the fertility of the soil are of no matter. Even in the case of farming while fertility may be a factor determining the kind of farming undertaken it is of far less importance than the location relative to customers and suppliers. A farm in a good location but with poor fertility will provide the opportunity for a better living than one with more fertile soil in a bad location. In a trading economy what matters in the general case is not the fertility of the soil but the advantages (externalities) available to a productive enterprise at a particular site. These advantages cannot give rise to a Ricardian rent for, as will be argued, they are produced by a combination of human and non-human factors. The essence of the Ricardian theory is that rent arises from a non-producible fixed factor.

The return to the factors of production in a trading economy is not, as is the case in a non-trading economy, a share of the output produced but a share of the income received from the sale of that output. There is a primary division of income rather than a primary division of output or wealth. The return to the human factor of production may be described as a *labour income* as it accrues to those who supply the necessary labour to the productive trading enterprise. The return to the non-human factors of production may be described as a *property income* because it accrues to those persons or corporate bodies who for the time being enjoy property rights over the non-human factors. The incomes commonly referred to as rent, interest or profit are sub-divisions of property income. However, what these factor incomes, or product shares, represent in real terms, will depend upon the relative market prices of the assortment of goods and services purchased out of those nominal incomes. For example, what labour income represents in real terms will depend on the price of what Pigou called 'wage goods' — the assortment of goods and services purchased out of labour incomes. Thus, assuming no change in nominal labour income, the share of the product accruing to those who supply labour will increase when the market price of wage goods falls and contract when the market price of wage goods rises. Market prices are of no significance in a non-trading economy but their influence permeates a trading economy.

Property Rights

The division of the net receipts from the sale of output between labour income and property income is the means by which a trading economy, through bargaining and market mechanisms, provides returns to the different factors of production. This primary division of income arises from the very nature of a trading economy. It follows that, to argue this division and the mechanisms by which it is achieved are the primal cause of the extremes of wealth and the other social diseases that appear endemic in contemporary trading economies, is to argue that these undesirable results also are in the nature of a free market trading economy. The argument accepts implicitly that in the nature of a trading economy 'the poor', in more senses than one, 'will always be with you'. The logical conclusion is that either the free market trading economy must be got rid of or attempts must be made to mitigate the undesirable results.

This conclusion has some apparent validity in certain circumstances. A free market allows property rights over the non-human factors of production to be accumulated in perpetuity into single holdings without limit. The same does not apply to the human factor, labour; the human effort any one person can make is strictly limited both in time and amount. Thus there arises the possibility of a concentration of property rights in the hands of a minority who, in order to produce an output, must become buyers of labour. The result is a society comprising a comparative few who are for ever growing richer and more powerful alongside the many who, having nothing to sell but their labour, are relatively poor. Some part of this majority is rendered poverty stricken when it is unable to sell its labour. This sequence of events is commonplace in contemporary trading economies and a matter of widespread concern, but so long as the cause remains, the result is unavoidable. The cause, however, does not lie in the nature of a trading economy: it is rooted in human failure, the failure of communities to conform to the principle of private property.

Except by fortunate accident, the primary division of income in a trading economy cannot result in what justice demands so long as the principle of private property is being flouted. John Stuart Mill in his *Principles of Political Economy* wrote, 'The laws of property have never yet conformed to the principles on which the justification of private property rests.'[1] This criticism continues to apply some 150 years later. The essential element of these principles, he wrote, 'consists in the recognition, in each person, of a right to the exclusive disposal of what he or she may have produced by their own exertions, or received by gift or fair agreement, without force or fraud, from those who produced it.'[2] Mill emphasised some of the consequences when members of trading economies fail to conform to this principle by custom, usage and law. Most of his remarks ring true today. Yet Mill's nineteenth century arguments couched in the Ricardian mode may mislead if applied directly to the present circumstances. Today landowners as a special class of persons are not, as Mill and many of his contemporaries implied they were in their day, the active culprits. Over the years the ownership of a title to land has become widespread and the majority of these landowners are more the passive acceptors of that to which by law they are entitled to receive and which the law allows them to keep in the most part for their own purposes. As Mill acknowledged it is governments who persistently fail in their duty to uphold the principle of private property and by their failure allow a few to exploit the economy for personal or corporate gain. Inflation, unemployment and the apparent general lack of justice which corrodes contemporary trading economies flow directly from the repetitive flouting by governments of the principle of private property.

Tax Revenue

In a trading economy both labour income and property income in the first instance accrue naturally as private income. Unless government has property rights over some or all of the non-human factors of production the primary division of income does not automatically provide a public revenue for financing necessary public expenditure. The common first reaction of governments to a lack of public revenue is to seek relief through the imposition of taxation. By whatever names taxes are called, or by whatever methods governments may use to raise tax revenue, taxation is in effect an arbitrary levy imposed by force or the threat of force (p.39) upon those in receipt of a private income. In their effective incidence all taxes are income taxes. By force of statutory law taxation denies to the individual taxpayer the right to the exclusive disposal of that individual's private income. Taxes either appropriate directly nominal private income, or erode real private income through rising prices, or, most often, both at once. Thus all taxation flouts the principle of private property. To describe taxes as customary duties, insurance, or (as happens in the preamble to the Annual Finance Act of the United Kingdom) 'gifts', is to use constitutional fiction in an attempt to obscure the nature of the act.

Governments, politicians and others put forward a wide variety of arguments in an attempt to justify the imposition of taxation. It is argued, for example, that progressive taxation offers the means for redistributing income from the rich to the poor. This argument may be sufficient to add morality to the medieval romance of Robin Hood but it does not add morality to the actions of twentieth century governments. In any event the evidence suggests that progressive taxation is ineffective for this purpose and that any redistribution achieved by governments flows from the expenditure side of the budget. In most cases taxation does little more than rob Peter to pay Paul what Paul could have better provided for himself had he also not been robbed in the first place. The various arguments put forward in an attempt to justify taxation may well be accepted by a majority of the electorate, a majority of the electorate may even appear to favour higher taxes for certain purposes, as the statistical wizards of some opinion polls claim, but none of this changes the nature of the act. With the imposition of taxation governments fail to conform to the principle of private property. Politicians may pay lip service to a 'property owning democracy', but when in power they misuse the force of statutory law and do not recognise in each person a right which is an essential element for the institution of private property. Trade is a matter of exchange, and fair exchange requires that each party to the exchange has and respects the valid title to whatever is exchanged. Any flouting of the principle of private property undermines the very foundations of a trading economy. Governments persistently flout this principle by the imposition of taxation.

The Road to a Mixed Economy

When governments become reliant upon tax revenue for the financing of public expenditure they cease to be subject to the discipline of having to adjust spending to income, a discipline that continues to apply to the private sector. The reverse discipline of adjusting income, that is tax revenue, to spending decisions has today become the accepted principle of public finance. United Kingdom governments, for example, take their spending decisions during the winter and to raise the necessary moneys present their budget the following spring.[3] This now unquestioned principle of public finance when allied to universal suffrage creates political pressures which work towards public profligacy. As the government's failure to uphold the principle of private property leads to extremes of wealth, this in turn sets up stresses and strains within the community and it appears to politicians they are faced with a choice. They may promise to do little or nothing and suffer the electoral consequences or they may offer some form of mitigating action. Mostly the freely elected governments of the developed trading economies have opted for mitigating action. At the outset this took the form of limited social and welfare schemes intended to relieve the worst excesses of social deprivation. However, the political pressures generated in these econo-mies by universal suffrage are such that this road has led, step by step and with the best of intentions, to the very expensive welfare state. In today's circumstances the need for some state welfare is all too apparent but to meet this need governments know of no alternative other than raising taxes. In other words governments, driven by political pressures and good intentions, attempt in their ignorance to spend their way out of trouble and to finance this spending by multiplying their tax take. The United Kingdom provides an example; tax revenue as a share of the net national product (NNP) at market prices has multiplied five fold dur-ing this century. A major part of this increase in tax has gone to finance the ever rising cost of establishing and attempting to sustain a welfare state. Yet the very circumstances that create the apparent need for extensive state welfare arise in the first place from the imposition of taxation.

As tax is an arbitrary levy on private income it cannot, regardless of political intentions, take fully into account an individual taxpayer's ability to pay. In the long run an ever increasing tax take tends in aggregate to squeeze disposable property income rather than disposable labour income. Again the United Kingdom provides an example. During this century the U.K. tax take has increased from between 8 to 9 per cent of net national product at market prices to over

40 per cent. Over the same period, while the share accruing as disposable labour income has fluctuated around a constant secular trend, the share accruing as disposable net property income has fallen from around 45 per cent of net national product at market prices to around 14 per cent. As property income is squeezed by taxation the firms in marginal industries sooner or later find themselves in a precarious financial position. Out of their disposable net income (all that is left out of income after meeting tax demands) they cannot pay an acceptable take-home pay to their employees, provide an acceptable return to those enjoying property rights over the firm itself and at the same time fund the investment necessary to remain competitive. As these threatened firms tend to be in industries basic to the well-being of the economy as a whole — agriculture, mining, railways and the like — in combination the firms have the power to demand and get some measure of protection (tariffs and the like) and financial support from government. By inhibiting trade, protection damages the whole of a trading economy while government financial support requires an increased tax take. Thus a course is set along a road upon which with every succeeding step economic and social difficulties are intensified and multiplied.

Along this road political pressures and the immediate needs of the economy eventually force governments into either taking over existing firms in a failing industry or allowing firms to go to the wall, setting up in their stead new state corporations. When this happens there is brought into existence what is called a 'mixed economy'. In a mixed economy some property rights over non-human factors of production are vested in the state and thus any property income that may accrue is a public income available to help fund public expenditure. However, the industries brought into the public sector in this way are mostly loss making firms who have failed, or who were in danger of failing, in the private sector. Governments find, therefore, that instead of being in receipt of a property income they are forced to increase public spending to pay an acceptable take-home pay to the new public employees and to provide funds for long overdue new investment. More public spending means an increased tax take and an increased tax take puts even more firms at risk. Once established, the public sector of mixed economies, like Topsy, 'just growed and growed'. As the public sector grows so also does the tax take.

The Reaction

For the quarter of a century following the end of World War II the elected governments of developed trading economies sought to mitigate social and economic afflictions by big government with extensive welfare schemes and a large public sector. Taxation was accepted not only as the means of raising the required public revenue, but also as an essential fiscal instrument for managing the economy. In general their approach was consistent with the policy prescriptions of the then dominant demand-side school of economic thought. When it became a fact of experience that this approach was failing and creating more troubles than it mitigated there came a reaction both in politics and in economic thought. The reactionary approach, consistent with the now dominant supply-side school of economic thought, requires the slimming down of government, the so-called 'targeting' of welfare schemes, a significant contraction of the public sector and a cut in the tax take. Unfortunately there is no evidence that any government has met the latter requirement to any significant extent. In any event the latest approach must fail, as did the earlier, so long as government remain ignorant of any acceptable alternative to persistently flouting the principle of private property by imposing taxation as the means of raising public revenue. Neither the old nor the new economic orthodoxy can offer enlightenment to government on this fundamental issue. As Ricardians note the primary division of wealth as between rent and wages, the later schools note the primary division of income as between labour income and property income, but fail to perceive further the special nature of a free market trading economy and, as a consequence, accept without question that public revenue means tax revenue. Worse, they accept also without question that the amount of tax revenue is to be determined by government spending decisions.

1. John S. Mill, *Principles of Political Economy*, Bk. II Ch. I para. 3.
2. *Ibid.* Bk. II Ch. II para. 1.
3. The present government (1993) are considering proposals for changing this order.

3

The General Theory
of Employment

In the conditions prevailing in contemporary industrialised trading economies, fiscal policy directed towards sustaining prosperity must take into account, amongst other things, the effects of government spending and taxation upon inflation, unemployment and international competitiveness. In these matters Keynes' general theory of employment is potentially a useful tool of analysis. First, by considering supply and demand together it allows the effects of demand-side policies to be distinguished from the effects supply-side policies. At one time demand-side policies may be appropriate, at another supply-side, at yet other times a combination of the two may be needed. Second, by assuming a short-run functional relationship between the volume of output and the amount of employment, the theory of Keynes treats output and employment as a single *dependent* variable. Thus, unlike the earlier 'classical' theory of employment it does not require the assumption of an automatic tendency towards full employment which is manifestly contrary to twentieth century experience. Nor does Keynes' theory require the assumption of an automatic tendency towards some exogenously determined 'natural rate of unemployment', as does contemporary monetarism. Indeed the monetarists' concept of a 'natural rate of unemployment' is not significantly different from the earlier concept of full employment as understood by what Keynes called the

'classical' economists. Third, the theory as formulated by
Keynes is described in terms of expected market prices and
so is relevant to the formulation of counter-inflationary
policies. Fourth, the use of the method of comparative statics
allows for an objective to be set relative to the current state
of an economy on to which the dynamics may be super-
imposed. Finally, as will be argued, developing Keynes'
theory leads to the logical conclusion that to sustain
prosperity and a high level of employment without such
side-effects as accelerating inflation, then government must
find an alternative to taxation as a means of raising public
revenue.

The substance of the theory as formulated by Keynes is
that any competitive economy tends towards a level of
activity determined by the point of intersection of an
aggregate demand function and an aggregate supply function. The aggregate supply price, Z, of the output of any
given amount of employment, N, is the expectation of
proceeds which will just make it worth the while of firms to
give that amount of employment. The aggregate supply
function, $Z = \Phi(N)$, expresses the relationship between Z
and N. The aggregate demand price, D, is the proceeds
firms expect to receive from the output of any given amount
of employment, N. The aggregate demand function, $D =
f(N)$, expresses the relationship between D and N. When the
value of D is greater than the value of Z firms will have an
incentive to expand and, conversely, when the value of D is
less than the value of Z firms will have an incentive to
contract. Thus, argued Keynes, an economy tends always
towards a level of activity at which the value of D equals the
value of Z. Keynes called the value of D at this point of
intersection 'the effective demand'. However, this is also the
point at which the value of Z equals the value of D and so
with equal validity may be called *the effective supply*. Had
Keynes used the term the effective supply rather than 'the
effective demand', and had he emphasised also 'the point of

true inflation' rather than an alternative term 'full employment' for the point where the aggregate supply price curve becomes vertical (p.25), then the later development and application of his theory may well have been significantly different. He was, of course, a man of his time, and in the 1930's demand and employment were the prime topics.

The Bargaining Mechanism

The concepts of aggregate demand price and aggregate supply price used by Keynes in his general theory of employment are developments in the Marshallian tradition and, therefore, take into account the basic process of bargaining. Any particular bargain is the result of an agreement between two parties and each party expects to gain from the exchange that follows. Bargaining is not a zero sum game. It is the expectation of gain that provides each party with the motivation for the trade. In a monetary economy the party bidding a money sum in exchange for the goods and/or services on offer is called, by convention, the buyer. The party offering goods and/or services in exchange for a money sum is called the seller. The money sum the buyer agrees to pay the seller is called the price.

As measured by the price, the point at which any particular bargain may be struck is confined within certain limits. The top limit, beyond which the price cannot rise, is determined by the buyer, who will have in mind a certain money sum in excess of which he is not prepared to strike a bargain with the seller for the goods and/or services on offer. At the top limit the buyer is indifferent. At any price below the top limit the buyer prefers the goods and/or services on offer to the money sum being asked. At any price above the top limit the buyer's preference is to hold the money sum rather than the goods and/or services on offer. The bottom limit, below which the price cannot fall, is determined by the seller who will have a certain money sum in mind below which he is not prepared to strike a bargain with the buyer for the goods and services on offer. At the bottom limit the seller is indifferent. At any price above the bottom limit the seller prefers the money to the goods and/or services offered. At any price below the bottom limit the seller prefers to keep the goods and/or services on offer rather than accept the money sum bid.

During the process of bargaining a buyer will know his top limit but will not know, and cannot know, the seller's bottom limit. The seller will know his bottom limit but will not know, and cannot know the buyer's top limit. Striking a bargain is possible only if there is a *bargaining gap*, that is where a buyer's top limit in money terms is, in the general case, greater than a seller's bottom limit expressed in the same money terms. Between these top and bottom limits the price at which a bargain is struck will depend on the bargaining skills and powers of the two parties. The importance of bargaining skills in affecting price is recognised by the many firms which employ specialist buyers and sellers. The most important bargaining power is the knowledge of the existence, or in the case of a monopoly the non-existence, of an alternative market.

The Aggregate Supply Price

In the special case of a bargaining process confined to a spot transaction, the bottom limit of the seller is indeterminate in the sense that it will depend solely on the seller's preferences at a given moment in a particular set of circumstances. In certain special circumstances a seller may even be prepared to make a money payment to the buyer. For example, a manufacturer, in order to dispose quickly of a piece of machinery for which he has no further use, may offer money as an additional inducement even though the machine is usable, not fully depreciated, and might be expected in different circumstances to command a positive market price.

In general, however, the bargaining process is part of the continuing or future production of an output and the bottom limit is determined by the money sum the seller expects will just make it worth while to produce the goods and services being offered. This money sum will be based on the seller's estimate of total cost including a minimum amount of profit. Thus, in line with Marshallian tradition (although not so specified by Keynes), the aggregate supply price of the output of a given amount of employment is an aggregate of the bottom limits of firms acting as sellers and considered as going concerns. Being an aggregate based on information known only to sellers it is a supply-side view of an economy. Given circumstances in which public expenditure is financed by taxation, then, consistent with the definition of Keynes, the aggregate supply price of the output of any given amount of employment is the proceeds firms expect will cover disposable labour income, or take-home pay, and total tax payments plus an amount of disposable profit just sufficient to induce firms to operate at that level of activity.

In Figure 1 the aggregate supply price is that described by an aggregate supply function $Z = \Phi(N)$. As is argued below, this curve is related, given the definition of aggregate supply price above, to an aggregate of total cost curves. It follows that at a level of activity corresponding to N_o average cost equals marginal cost[1] and, therefore, at this point average cost is at a minimum. For an economy as a whole the level of activity at which average cost is minimised is also that at which the general price level will be lowest consistent with an expectation of profit just sufficient to induce that level of activity. In this sense such a level of activity may be considered as coinciding with the optimum utilization of existing capacity. At any level of activity to the left of N_o marginal cost is less than average cost and existing capacity is, in general, under-utilized. In the other direction at any level of activity to the right of N_o marginal cost is higher than average cost and existing capacity is, in general,

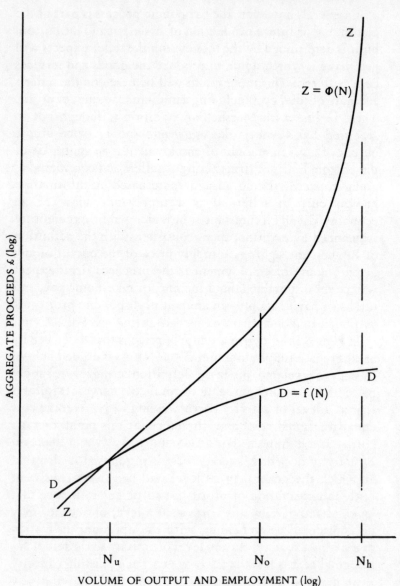

VOLUME OF OUTPUT AND EMPLOYMENT (log)

Figure 1

over-utilized. Thus at any level of activity less than the optimum — to the left of N_o in Figure 1 — an expansion of activity up to the optimum would be associated with a falling general price level. Further expansion beyond the optimum — to the right of N_o in Figure 1 — will be associated with a general price level rising at an ever accelerating rate. At a level of activity corresponding to a vertical aggregate supply price curve — N_h on Figure 1 — further expansion is impossible in the prevailing conditions, and any additional aggregate monetary demand will be fully absorbed by rising prices. Keynes called this point 'a state of true inflation'[2], but it is more in the nature of a supply horizon. From a supply-side point of view N_h is as far as may be seen in the short-run during which existing capacity is a fixed factor limiting the expansion of output. In the longer-run the supply horizon is not fixed, but will move to the left or right as firms vary their investment or dis-investment in capacity, depending upon their expectations on the future course of business.

The Aggregate Demand Price

In any particular bargaining process the top limit of the buyer is indeterminate since, like the seller's bottom limit in the case of spot transactions (p. 22), it depends solely on the buyer's preferences at a particular moment in a given set of circumstances. However, this is irrelevant to Keynes' theory as the aggregate demand price is not an aggregate based on the top limits of buyers (p. 21) but, as stated above (p. 20), the proceeds *firms expect to receive* from the output of a given amount of employment. In other words, it is an aggregate of the net receipts from the per unit prices firms expect buyers to pay for a given quantity of output. Thus the aggregate demand price, like the aggregate supply price, is derived from a supply-side view of the bargaining process. From this supply-side view the aggregate supply price is an

aggregate of sellers' bottom limits but the aggregate demand
price is not, and cannot be, an aggregate of buyers' top
limits, for this requires information that sellers, having a
supply-side only view, cannot know.

In a closed economy the aggregate demand price is widely
accepted to be the sum of expected consumer spending,
investment spending and general government spending on
final consumption (C+I+G). The standard system of
national accounting conforms to this definition. This is
useful for demand management, but the acceptance of this
definition results in the component parts of the aggregate
demand price being unrelated to the component parts of the
aggregate supply price as defined above (p.23). A corres-
pondence of component parts consistent with the supply-
side view taken by Keynes for his general theory of employment (p.20) requires spending on consumption and investment (C+I) to be re-defined to include only spending out of
take-home pay and disposable net profit components of the
aggregate supply price. General government spending (G)
may be then defined as spending out of tax revenue plus
general government borrowing requirement. An advantage
of redefining the theory in this way is that general
government propensity to spend out of tax revenue plus
borrowing requirement is, by definition, always equal to
unity.

In Figure 1 the aggregate demand price curve is that
described by an aggregate demand function $D = f(N)$. The
point of intersection between the two functions is drawn to
correspond with a level of activity N_u, implying slumpy
conditions in which existing capacity is generally under-
utilized and, as a result, firms are confronted by an inelastic
demand price curve. To the right of any point of intersection
the theory of Keynes predicts the aggregate demand price
curve to be less elastic than the aggregate supply price curve.
At a level of activity to the left of that corresponding to N_o,
the economy as a whole is subject to decreasing average cost.

In the case illustrated therefore the economy must, by derivation from the aggregate supply price, be faced with an inelastic aggregate demand price curve. An economy will be faced with an elastic demand price curve only when subject to increasing average cost with the point of intersection to the right of a level of activity corresponding to N_o and approaching the supply horizon N_h. As the aggregate demand price curve is not limited by the supply horizon, it is shown in Figure 1 as cutting the perpendicular N_h.

A Supply-Side View

The view of an economy as a whole as illustrated by Figure 1 is a supply-side view — the view of sellers, or producers, or firms. That this is a supply-side view is important. It is the fact of this view which refutes the argument that, as there cannot be more than one market price, there is a logical contradiction in the assumption that both the aggregate demand price and the aggregate supply price represent the expectations of firms. For example, Pantinkin argues that at any level of activity to the left of a point of intersection, say N_u in Figure 2, firms expect two different per unit prices: one corresponding to the aggregate supply price $N_u Z$ and the other corresponding to the aggregate demand price $N_u D$. This argument ignores the fact of a supply-side only point of view. Firms, as suppliers, can view an economy only from the supply-side. For firms the aggregate demand price $N_u D$ (Figure 2) is the proceeds they expect to receive from the output of a given amount of employment N_u. The aggregate demand price $N_u D$ corresponds then to the per unit market prices firms expect buyers will pay for that particular quantity of output which would be the outcome of their giving an amount of employment N_u. The aggregate supply price $N_u Z$ (Figure 2) is not an expected market price, but corresponds to the per unit prices firms expect will yield, at that level of activity, proceeds just sufficient to cover total costs, including a minimum profit. The expectations of proceeds N_uZ is sufficient to induce firms to produce the output of an amount of employment N_u, but in the given conditions of demand they expect to receive more for that quantity of output; they expect to receive N_uD. In other words, in the market conditions illustrated by Figure 2 and operating at a level of activity N_u, firms expect proceeds to yield a profit in excess of that which would just make it worth their while to produce an output of an amount of employment N_u.

At any level of activity the total of the per unit market prices firms expect buyers to pay for a given output corresponds always to the aggregate demand price. Only at the point of intersection, where the value of D equals the value of Z, does the total of expected per unit market prices of output correspond also to the aggregate supply price. Indeed it is that which, according to Keynes' theory, stops an economy tending automatically towards the supply horizon, the point Keynes called 'full employment' or 'a state of true inflation'. At any level of activity to the right of a point of intersection the value of D is less than the value of Z, which implies a circumstance where the per unit market prices firms expect buyers to pay will yield a profit insufficient to induce them to operate at such a level of activity.

Profit

In a firm's accounts profit is a residual item. This profit is a money sum that has actually accrued to a firm during a given time period and, in the accounting sense of a money sum actually realised, it is realistic to assume an individual firm to be a profit maximising organisation. It is in the interests of every firm to endeavour to ensure that its realised profit during a given time period is the best possible that can be achieved in the competitive conditions within which it operates. As Adam Smith stated, 'It is not from the

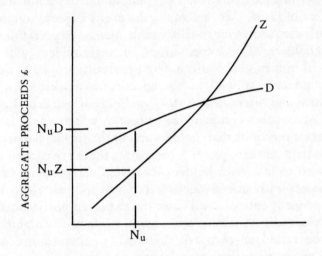

VOLUME OF OUTPUT AND EMPLOYMENT

Figure 2

benevolence of the butcher, the brewer, or the baker, that we expect our dinner, but from their regard for their own interest. We address ourselves not to their humanity, but to their self-love; and never talk to them of our own necessities, but of their own advantages'.[3] However, profit is, in the accounting sense, a result, and while firms in their own interests may be assumed to strive for the best possible results, the production for sale is a risk-taking activity and for an individual firm that result may be a loss. Whether the accounting result is a gain or loss, it is not the profit that enters into the aggregate supply price as this is a certain sum the expectation of which is just sufficient to induce firms in aggregate to operate at a particular level of activity.

The amount of profit, the expectation of which is just sufficient to induce a firm to operate at any given level of activity in a particular line of production, is determined by a variety of factors. For example, the profit expectation must be sufficient to cover the disposable income expectations of shareholders. The expectations of shareholders will be related in turn to the alternative oportunities open to those shareholders, as well as to the current market view in national and international stock and capital markets. In the case of a quoted company the extent to which it fulfills the expectations of its shareholders and of the financial markets will affect its share price. A company's share price cannot be allowed to fall much below the current market price of its net assets without endangering its continued existence as an independent entity. In all cases the expected profit must be sufficient also to ensure that capital funds are available, or can be raised on competitive terms, to finance any new investment necessary to maintain the firm's competitive edge. Thus for every firm there is a minimum profit which is in the nature of a cost and which, taking one year with another, must be covered by the expected proceeds from its output of a given amount of employment if the firm is to continue to give that amount of employment.

In a competitive market economy any firm, or group of firms in combination, which attempts to achieve a profit much in excess of a necessary minimum by restricting output and raising prices must expect to encourage competitors and thus suffer a loss of market share. For example, the OPEC policy of raising the price of crude oil by restricting the output of its members encouraged exploration and production in non-member countries throughout the world and so led to a loss of market share for OPEC members. Apart from exceptional cases of monopoly or near monopoly the fear of additional competition and loss of market share will overcome the attraction of a short-run 'fast buck'. All firms must act 'with regard to their own interest', as Adam Smith recognised, and to this extent individual firms may be considered to be profit maximising organisations. Taking the longer view, however, what is effectively a maximum profit in competitive conditions for an individual firm is related not to the point where its marginal cost equals marginal revenue but to the point where its total cost, including a minimum profit, equals its total revenue. The competitive struggle in which all firms are engaged in an open trading economy causes them to drive each other towards a level of activity at which they can expect both individually and in aggregate no more than an amount of profit just sufficient to induce that activity. It is this necessary minimum amount of expected profit that is, for individual firms and for firms in aggregate, in the nature of a cost which is the profit included within the aggregate supply price.

By definition (pp.20, 23) all points on the aggregate supply price curve are points at which the expected disposable net profit is the minimum needed to induce firms to operate at that particular level of activity. Therefore the point of inter-section between the aggregate demand function and the aggregate supply function is also a point of minimum profit. Moreover, at any level of activity in excess of that corres-ponding to the point of intersection, for example, to the right of N_u in Figure 1, profit will be less than firms need to induce such a level of activity. In the opposite direction any level of activity less than that corresponding to the point of intersection, for example to the left of N_u in Figure 1, the expected profit will be, as the value of Z is less than the value of D, in excess of that minimum needed to induce firms to operate at that level of activity. Thus the general theory of employment predicts that in the short-run, during which existing conditions and capacity are fixed factors, an expan-sion of activity will tend always to be associated for firms in general with a smaller profit or greater loss. On the same assumptions the theory predicts for firms in general a contraction of activity to be associated in the short-run always with a tendency towards an expected larger profit or smaller loss.

Keynes' assertion that the point of intersection is the 'point that entrepreneurs' expectation of profits will be maximised' is inconsistent with his definitions and with predictions from his theory based on those definitions.[4] His assertion is consistent only providing the aggregate demand price curve and the aggregate supply price curve are aggregates of marginal revenue and marginal cost curves as illustrated in the top half of Figure 3. However, Keynes defined both the aggregate demand price and the aggregate supply price in terms of 'the proceeds' which he used as a convenient shorthand for 'the aggregate income (i.e. factor cost plus profit)'.[5] He did not use the words *additional* or *marginal* proceeds which would imply aggregates based on marginal revenue and marginal cost. Thus his aggregate demand price must be taken as an aggregate of *total* net revenue and his aggregate supply price as an aggregate of total net cost including a minimum profit. This is a level of revenue containing profit 'which will just make it worth while of the entrepreneurs to give that employment'.[6] Such a profit can be interpreted therefore only as a minimum. If firms in aggregate are assumed to be profit maximisers, then Keynes' theory predicts that an economy will tend automatically to contract away from the point of intersection at which the effective aggregate demand price and the effective aggregate supply price have the same value. As illustrated on Figure 3, individual firms, when considered as profit maximising organisations, tend to contract from the level of activity, indicated by the minimum profit vertical, determined by the intersection of total cost and total revenue curves, towards the maximum profit vertical, determined by the point of intersection of the marginal cost and marginal revenue curves. It follows therefore that, for an economy as a whole to tend automatically towards a level

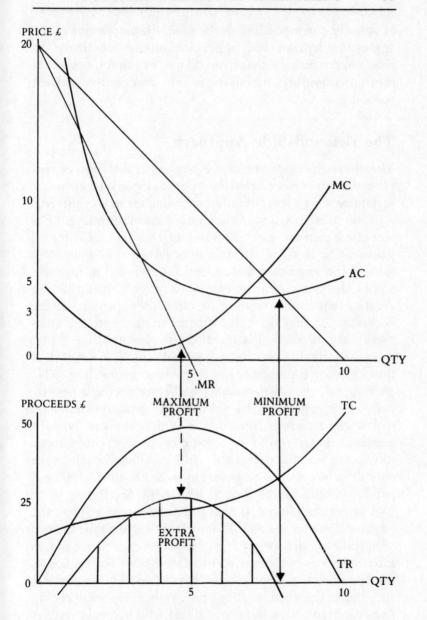

Figure 3

of activity corresponding to the point of intersection of the aggregate demand and aggregate supply functions, the requirement must be that firms do not, or cannot, operate as profit maximising organisations in a competitive market economy.

The Demand-Side Approach

The above development of Keynes' general theory of employment gives some limited support to those who advocate sustaining a high level of public spending as the way towards a prosperous economy. When government spending, G, is increased then *cet. par.*, the value of D is increased for all values of N. In Figure 1 this is the equivalent of an upward shift of the aggregate demand price curve and in turn this causes the point of intersection to move to the right so creating conditions tending to cause an expansion of the economy. At first sight this appears an easy option but the theory also predicts that travelling too long and too far on this road is likely to create as many difficulties as it solves. If the expansion is pushed beyond a point corresponding to N_0 on Figure 1, then the economy will be subject to a persistently rising general price level and home producers will tend to lose their competitive edge in both home and overseas markets. Again, given circumstances where government rely on tax revenue to finance public spending then there are only three ways open to government to raise the additional public revenue and all have deleterious side-effects.

A government may, as Milton Friedman put it, print the additional money needed. That this method of public finance soon leads to inflation is a fact of repeated experience and, as inflationary expectations spread throughout the economy, the last state is worse than the first. The additional public spending is absorbed in rising prices rather than encouraging expansion and so inflation is added to whatever troubles existed at the outset. Another option open to government is to increase the tax take. With this method of financing additional public spending the increase in taxation, T, tends to increase the value of Z for all values of N. In Figure 1 this represents an upward shift of the aggregate supply price curve in step with the upward shift of the aggregate demand price curve. As these two curves rise together the point of intersection rises nearly vertically, leading to rising prices with little or no expansion of activity. Unless the money supply is increased as prices rise then, very quickly, the rise in prices will be followed by a contraction of activity. Yet again, the theory predicts that this method of financing public spending results in the last state being worse than the first.

The remaining option open to government is for them to finance their additional spending by borrowing. The eventual outcome of this method depends to a large extent on the particular circumstances at the time and the precise method by which government borrows. When government borrowing is no more than a method of increasing the money supply it is really printing money and this leads directly to inflation with the consequences noted above. When government borrowing conforms to what Milton Friedman and others call 'true borrowing' then the borrowing will not be a direct cause of inflation, although it may cancel out any expansionary tendencies motivated by the additional public spending. This cancelling out will happen when the funds borrowed by government would have been spent otherwise by the private sector. As public spending financed by true borrowing increases, private sector spending on investment is squeezed out and so there is little or no net effect on aggregate demand. Only when government is borrowing 'idle balances', generated by an economy's propensity to save being greater than its propensity to invest, will the financing of public spending by true borrowing have the intended expansionary impulse without the addition of unwelcome side-effects. This kind of operation is often

called a pump priming measure which may be expected to
jerk an economy out of a prolonged depression. Such a policy
was advocated by Maynard Keynes and other leading economists during the early thirties as a way out of that particular
depression. At the time it was called 'deficit spending on
public works'. Nonetheless, even in the appropriate circumstances the policy is no more than a once and for all measure
which cannot be sustained. As an economy begins to expand
then the generation of idle balances will decrease as the
propensity to invest increases to equate with the propensity
to save. As this continues true borrowing by government
will begin to squeeze out private sector investment spending
and cease to have its original expansionary effect. Keynes'
general theory of employment supports a policy of increased
public spending by deficit financing only in certain circumstances and as a short-run pump priming measure.

The Supply-Side Approach

The development of Keynes' general theory of employment
provides also some support for supply-side tax cutting
policies. When a government cuts its tax take then the value
of T is reduced and this tends to reduce the value of Z for all
values of N. In Figure 1 this represents a downward shift of
the aggregate supply price curve which will, *cet. par.*, shift
the point of intersection to the right and so tend to expand
the economy. However, the *cet. par.* qualification assumes
no significant change in the aggregate demand price curve,
but this is unlikely unless public spending, G, is also unchanged. It is unlikely since, although a cut in tax take will
increase the private sector's disposable income, the private
sector's propensity to spend out of disposable income, is
usually less than government's propensity to spend out of tax
revenue. The qualification assumes also that public spending
is sustained without incurring a deficit to be met by printing
money or borrowing. In certain circumstances given an open

economy this latter assumption may be realistic. A reduction in the value of Z for all values of N allows home producers to become more competitive as against overseas producers and thus create a tendency for exports, E, to increase not only absolutely but also relative to imports, M. An improvement in exports and a reduction in imports may be expected to compensate for some cut in public spending without causing a reduction in aggregate demand. Further, as most of any expansion will be reflected in home produced incomes this will lead to buoyant tax revenues which in turn will assist in preventing a deficit.

Since Keynes' theory predicts that a cut in the tax take will reduce the value of Z for all values of N, then the logical conclusion is that an open market economy can attain the lowest possible aggregate supply price in given conditions only when all domestic taxes are abolished. When the value of Z for all values of N is the lowest possible, then home producers have the opportunity to be most competitive in both home and overseas markets. Only when home producers are highly competitive in world markets can an open free market economy be properous and sustain a high level of activity. The weakness of Keynes' theory is that, while leading to such a conclusion, it does not offer a solution to the issue of raising the necessary public revenue without recourse to taxation. The strength of Keynes' theory is that it does isolate the fundamental difficulty facing contemporary trading economies; this is that taxation must, sooner rather than later, inflate the aggregate supply price and so lead inevitably to a loss of competitiveness, rising prices and rising unemployment. The theory serves also as an analytical tool for discovering the processes by which taxation affects both prices and unemployment. An understanding of these processes is a prerequisite for the formulation and implementation of effective policies designed to remedy the defects which today appear to be inherent in free market open economies.

1. Since Figure 1 is on a log-log scale, marginal cost equals average cost at a point where the aggregate supply price curve is tangental to a line of 45 degrees sloping upwards to the right.
2. J. M. Keynes, *The General Theory of Employment, Interest and Money*, p.119.
3. Adam Smith, *The Wealth of Nations*, Bk.I, Ch.II.
4. Keynes, *op. cit.* p.25.
5. *Ibid.* p.24.
6. *Ibid.* p.24.

4
Tax Analysis

Economic theorists hold, with reasonable consistency, that the essence of a tax is the absence of a direct *quid pro quo* between the taxpayer and the public authority. It is this that distinguishes a tax from other charges that may be imposed by a public authority. A useful definition is provided by Hugh Dalton: 'a tax is a compulsory contribution imposed by a public authority, irrespective of the exact amount of service rendered to the taxpayer in return, and not imposed as a penalty for any legal offence'.[1] This definition is not a classification of individual taxes and does not rest on the shifting sands of what, for one purpose or another, is from time to time 'always called taxes' or 'never called taxes'. Excluded is public authority revenue from public property and from the pricing policies of state owned enterprises. Revenue derived from public property and state owned enterprises is not different in kind from private income derived from private property and private enterprise. A so-called 'monopoly tax' imposed by a state owned monopoly is not different in kind from a 'monopoly tax' imposed by a privately owned monopoly. On the other hand the definition includes, for example, what today are called 'national insurance contributions' or 'social security contributions'. In particular Dalton's definition is useful since taxation enters into the aggregate supply price for the reason that it is 'a compulsory contribution imposed by a public authority' and is not a payment for 'the exact amount of service rendered to the taxpayer in return'.

The adminstrative classification of taxes which is used by most writers on public finance is no tool for economic analysis. This method of classification is based on the assumption that tax incidence accords with the intentions of the taxing authorities. A tax is classified as a 'direct tax' because the taxing authority intends it to be paid by the person who receives the income upon which the tax is assessed. Likewise with social security contributions: employee contributions are intended to be paid by employees, while employer contributions are intended to be paid by employers. A tax is classified as an 'indirect tax', or expenditure tax, when the taxing authority intends that tax to be passed on to the final consumer by way of higher prices. For example, excise duty on beer is classified as an indirect tax because the taxing authority intend the tax to be passed on from the brewer to the publican as a price increase and to be passed on yet again by the publican as a price increase to the final purchaser. At this superficial level the administrative classification appears to conform with the facts of experience. Consumers know as a fact of experience that price rises are often justified by, and follow closely upon, increases in indirect taxation and thus the tax inflated price appears to fulfill the intentions of the taxing authorities. Employees are reminded regularly of 'direct taxation' by the difference between gross pay and take-home pay printed on their pay slips. To them this tax wedge appears to reduce directly what otherwise would accrue to them as disposable income. However, in the case of taxation what appears to be is not what is.

To politicians the administrative classification of taxes has an obvious attraction. It carries the implicit assumption that tax incidence accords with their intentions. This allows tax changes to be justified by slogans. Awkward questions relating to tax increases may be avoided by claiming to 'tax the rich to help the poor', 'redistribute incomes', and so on. Again, depending upon whether one is supporting or opposing the government, tax cuts may be presented as 'making the rich richer', 'extending the freedom of choice', 'letting the money fructify in the pockets of the people' and so on.

The media refer to a tax cutting budget as 'a give-away budget' which may sound a pleasing note but is akin to describing a burglary where some valuables have been left behind as a 'give-away burglary'. Nonetheless, these and similar slogans do not prevent the expressed good intentions of politicians being thwarted in practice. The intended payers of a tax can and do retaliate, while those expecting a 'gift' from the Chancellor of the Exchequer usually end up empty handed or worse. In matters of fiscal policy the administrative classification of taxes assists the creation of political myths and provides a fine facade which obscures fiscal injustice.

An Alternative Classification

Sir John and Lady Ursula Hicks have provided an alternative framework for tax analysis by distinguishing between the *formal incidence* and the *effective incidence* of a tax. In most cases the formal and effective incidence do not coincide but are linked through both time and space by the process of *tax shifting*.[2] The formal incidence of a tax refers to the initial impact of the tax. For example, an increase in social security contributions of employees reduces their take-home pay immediately and directly by the amount of the increase. The reduction in take-home pay is the measure of the formal incidence of the increase in that particular tax. Elsewhere Lady Ursula points out that the calculation of the formal incidence says nothing of the taxpayer's reaction or of its consequences. In the *Economic Journal* she used Panteleoni's metaphor of a stone being thrown into a pond.[3] The formal incidence of a tax is taken as analogous to the plop of the stone as it breaks the surface of the pond. This stone will set up an ever widening circle of ripples disturbing the surface and eventually causing some damage to the banks. The ripples are analogous to the tax shifting process and the damage to the banks is analogous to the effective incidence. Lady Ursula emphasises that tax analysis needs to be able to trace the whole sequence of events. For example, retaliation to a tax-imposed cut in take-home pay by demands for higher gross pay will set off a tax shifting process. This tax shifting process upsets the equilibrium of firms and markets as it continues to where the tax burden finally comes to rest, at the place of the *effective* incidence of that tax.

The sequence that follows upon a stone being thrown into a pond is useful in illustrating the operation of a particular tax through the economic system. But the analogy has limitations and these often lead those engaged in tax analysis to attempt the impossible — with misleading conclusions. In the economic pond there is not one stone, one ever widening circle of ripples leading eventually to some damage to the banks of the pond. There are a multitude of stones being thrown into the economic pond continuously; the ripples cross and recross, combine, separate , re-combine, separate yet again and reach the banks only to rebound and cause further disturbance. As it is impossible to trace the disturbance caused by one stone out of a multitude, so also it is impossible to trace any one of many taxes from its formal incidence through the process of tax shifting to its effective incidence, the place where the tax shifting process stops. With the shifting process tax effects merge; as they merge the effects of one tax becomes indistinguishable from the effects of many others, or even from the effects of the tax system as a whole. Thus, while the distinction between the formal and effective incidence provides a framework that enables tax analysis to take into account the whole process of tax shifting, the classification of taxes has of necessity to be based on the formal incidence of a tax. Once the effect of one tax merges with the effects other taxes, classification is not only impossible but meaningless.

In their formal incidence all taxes create a tax liability and tax liability is, in common with other liabilities, a component part of the aggregate supply price (p.23). However, not all taxes in their formal incidence cause a change in the aggregate supply function, that is, cause a change in the value of Z for all values of N. The formal incidence of an increase in employees' social security contributions, for example, will increase tax liability and simultaneously reduce take-home pay by a money sum equivalent to the increase in tax. Thus in its formal incidence the imposition of, or change in, employees' social security contributions will not cause a change in the aggregate supply function. Any increase/decrease in employees' tax liability is simultaneously offset by a decrease/increase in take-home pay and, *cet.par.*, the value of Z remains unchanged for all values of N. On the other hand, the formal incidence of an increase in employers' social security contributions will increase the tax liability of firms, but will not cause an offsetting decrease in other component parts of the aggregate supply price. Thus by its formal incidence the imposition of, or change in, employers' social security contributions will cause a change in the aggregate supply function. The value of Z will be changed for all values of N by precisely the same money sum as the amount of the tax change and with the same sign.

The distinction made by Sir John and Lady Hicks in conjunction with Keynes' general theory of employment provides a useful alternative to the administrative classification of taxes. Particular taxes can be classified on the basis of the effect of their formal incidence on the aggregate supply function. When the formal incidence of a particular tax does not cause a change in the aggregate supply function, it will be classified in this text as an *income-effect* tax. Similarly when the formal incidence of a particular tax is the cause of a change in the aggregate supply function, it will be classified as a *supply-effect* tax. In many cases this macroeconomic method of classifying taxes cuts across administrative classifications. For example, local rates in the United Kingdom were assumed to inflate the current market price for renting dwellings and business premises and, as a result, classified as taxes on expenditure in accordance with the administrative classification of taxes. Using the classification based on the effect of the formal incidence upon the aggregate supply function, domestic local rates were an income-effect tax. In their formal incidence they could have no impact effect on the aggregate supply function. Local rates on business premises were a supply-effect tax. By their formal incidence they directly affected a firm's costs and as a result caused a change in the aggregate supply function. Similarly the new Council Tax to be levied on domestic householders is an income-effect tax, while the new Uniform Business Rate is a supply-effect tax.

The Formal Incidence

The analysis of the formal incidence of a change in taxation implies a run short enough to preclude the possibility of retaliation by taxpayers. This is to say there is no possibility of a tax shifting process being motivated. Such an analysis casts doubts on the conventional wisdom of demand management techniques in so far as their immediate effects on an economy are concerned. Demand management techniques are based on the assumption that any increase in the amount of taxation is always contractionary, deflationary, or both, and any cut in the amount of taxation is always expansionary, or inflationary, or both. For example, in the practice of demand management an increase in those taxes included within what was formerly called 'the regulator' is held to be counter-inflationary. The policy intention is to 'take the heat out of the economy' by a tax-induced rise in prices leading to a cut-back in aggregate real demand; this is to say that an increase in tax intended to raise prices is both contradictary and, paradoxically, counter-inflationary. However, analysis based on the formal incidence of changes in the amount of taxation leads to the conclusion that in the short-run at least the assumptions inherent in demand management techniques do not always hold in the real world. There are many circumstances in which the impact of a change in the amount of taxation will produce immediate results precisely opposite

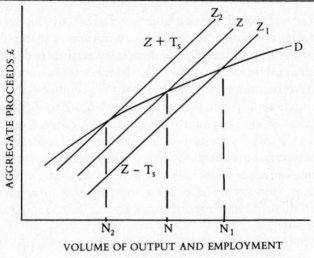

VOLUME OF OUTPUT AND EMPLOYMENT

Figure 4

to those predicted and intended by the advocates of demand management. In any period of time short enough to preclude tax shifting the result produced by the formal incidence of any change in the amount of taxation will depend on a number of factors, such as government's propensity to spend out of tax revenue, the relationship of this propensity to the rest of the economy's propensity to spend out of their disposable income, whether the tax change applies to income-effect or supply-effect taxes, the elasticities of the relevant sections of the aggregate demand price and aggregate supply price schedules and the elasticity of the money supply.

The formal incidence of a change in the amount of supply-effect taxation causes an immediate change in the aggregate supply function since, by definition, there is a change in the value of Z for all values of N. The change in the aggregate supply function will cause in turn (assuming an unchanged aggregate demand function) a shift in the point of intersection. As illustrated in Figure 4 a cut in supply-effect taxation by an amount $-T_s$ shifts the aggregate supply price curve downwards from Z to Z_1 and the point of intersection to the right, corresponding to a higher level of activity N_1. Such an expansionary policy is, on these assumptions, counter-inflationary and most likely to be associated with a tendency for the general price level to fall. Conversely an increase in supply-effect taxation by an amount $+ T_s$ (Figure 4) shifts the aggregate supply price curve upwards from Z to Z_2, causing the point of intersection to move to the left corresponding to a lower level of activity N_2. In most cases the contraction of activity will be associated with a rising general price level, but in some cases, especially when the money supply is highly inelastic, the supply-effect tax increase may precipitate a slump of sufficient intensity to lead to a fall in the general price level.

Whether the formal incidence of a change in supply-effect taxation affects the aggregate demand function will depend largely on the government's marginal propensity to spend out of tax revenue. The change in taxation will not, in its formal incidence, cause a change in non-government disposable incomes, but it will cause a change in the non-government sector's expected tax liability. What from the point of view of firms is a change in expected tax liability is from governments' viewpoint a change in expected tax revenue. If the government's marginal propensity to spend out of tax revenue is equal to zero, then the aggregate demand function is likely to remain unchanged and the formal incidence of a cut in supply-effect taxation will provide an expansionary impulse, while an increase will provide a contractionary impulse. When government's marginal propensity to spend is greater than zero, then it is to be expected that government spending will change to some extent in line with the change in tax liabilty. A cut in supply-effect taxation will be associated with a cut in government spending, while an increase will be associated with an increase in government spending. In these circumstances the formal incidence of the tax change will cause the aggregate demand function to change in a way that will reduce the tax effect on

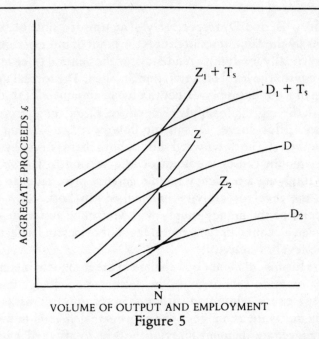

Figure 5

the level of activity and increase the tax effect on the general price level. When government's marginal propensity to spend out of tax revenue is equal to unity then, given a sufficiently elastic money supply, the formal incidence of a change in the amount of supply-effect taxation will affect the general level of prices and leave the level of activity in the economy as a whole largely unchanged. A cut in supply-effect taxes will tend to reduce prices and an increase will tend to raise prices. Within this overall result there will be some disturbance as a consequence of the expected change in government demand, or government induced demand, relative to non-government demand.

In Figure 5 the government's marginal propensity to spend out of tax revenue is assumed to be equal to unity. Thus, the formal incidence of an increase in supply-effect tax by an amount $+ T_s$ results in both the aggregate supply price curve, Z, and the aggregate demand price curve, D, shifting upwards to Z_1 and D_1 respectively. The upward shift of both curves by the same amount causes the point of intersection to rise vertically implying a tendency for the general price level to rise with the level of activity unchanged. The formal incidence of a cut in supply-effect tax by an amount $-T_s$ results in both the aggregate supply price curve, Z, and the aggregate demand price curve, D, shifting downwards to Z_2 and D_2 respectively. The downward shift of both these curves by the same amount causes the point of intersection to fall vertically implying a tendency for the general price level to fall with the level of activity unchanged. In both cases the elasticity of the money supply will determine any trade-off between a change in the general level of prices and a change in the level of activity.

The formal incidence of a change in the amount of income-effect taxation cannot cause, by definition, a change in the aggregate supply function, although in certain circumstances it may motivate a change in the aggregate demand function. The aggregate demand function will be unaffected by the formal incidence of a change in the amount of income-effect tax only when government's marginal propensity to spend out of tax revenue is equal to the non-government sector's propensity to spend out of disposable income. Given this circumstance any increase/decrease in government's expected spending will be fully offset by a decrease/increase in non-government expected spending. When government's marginal propensity to spend out of tax revenue is greater than the rest of the economy's marginal propensity to spend out of their disposable income, then the formal incidence of an increase in the amount of income-effect tax will tend to increase aggregate demand price. Although government expected tax revenue will increase by the same amount as the rest of the economy's expected disposable income is reduced, the government's expected spending will rise by more than the non-government sector's expected spending falls. Thus the aggregate demand price curve will shift upwards as the

value of D is increased for all values of N and the point of
intersection will move to the right consistent with an expansion of the economy. Likewise in the same circumstances the
formal incidence of a cut in the amount of income-effect tax
will tend to contract activity. The increase in the non-
government sector's expected spending out of their additional disposable income will not fully offset the fall in
government's expected spending out of a smaller tax
revenue. As the value of D falls for all values of N the aggregate demand price curve will shift downwards and the point
of intersection move to the left consistent with a contraction
of activity.

When government's propensity to spend out of tax
revenue is less than the rest of the economy's propensity to
spend out of their disposable income then the tendencies
described in the preceding paragraph are reversed. The
formal incidence of an increase in income-effect tax will
tend to contract activity. The rise in government's expected
spending out of an increased tax revenue will be less than
sufficient to offset the fall in the non-government sector's
expected spending out of their reduced disposable income.
As the value of D falls for all values of N the aggregate
demand price curve will shift downwards causing the point
of intersection to move to the left, consistent with a contraction of activity. Given the same relationship between pro-
pensities to spend between the government and non-government sectors, the formal incidence of a cut in the amount of
income-effect tax will tend to expand an economy. The rise
in non-government expected spending out of an increased
disposable income will more than offset the fall in government's expected spending out of a smaller tax revenue. As the
value of D increases for all values of N, the aggregate
demand price curve will shift upwards, causing the point of
intersection to move to the right, consistent with an expansion of activity.

The formal incidence of supply-effect taxation directly

inflates the aggregate supply price and this automatically motivates a process of tax shifting which tends to raise prices, or to contract output and employment, or to some combination of these two. With income-effect taxation the process of tax shifting is motivated only when the taxpayer retaliates against the imposition of the tax. When the amount, or change in the amount, of income-effect tax is insufficient to cause the taxpayer to retaliate, or when the taxpayer cannot retaliate, then the formal incidence is also the effective incidence of the tax. Adam Smith, for example, argued that the receivers of ground rents cannot shift a tax imposed on their rental income. In contemporary economic theory it is accepted in general that a tax imposed on monopoly or rental incomes cannot be shifted. However, in most cases the formal incidence of an income-effect tax does cause a taxpayer to retaliate and this sets in motion a process of tax shifting. Once this process is motivated, whether directly by the imposition of the tax or by the retaliation of taxpayers, it will continue until either the effect of the tax is shifted upon incomes whose recipients cannot retaliate, or the amount of the tax becomes so diffused throughout the economy as to become insufficient at any one point to cause further retaliation. The process of tax shifting results in a significant difference between the formal and effective incidence of a tax. Indeed, where tax incidence finally comes to rest is a matter of chance and is unlikely, except by accident, to accord with any policy intention. Of even greater importance for individuals, firms and the well-being of an economy as a whole, is the fact that the tax shifting process is the cause of much disturbance and distortion throughout the economy and in particular is a significant primal cause of rising prices and unemployment.

1. Hugh Dalton, *Principles of Public Finance.*
2. *The Incidence of Local Rates in Great Britain*, National Institute of Economic and Social Research.
3. *Economic Journal*, Vol.LVI no.221, March 1946.

5

Tax and Inflation

Any amount of taxation results in a higher general price level than would be the case without that amount of tax. Any cut in the amount of existing taxation results eventually in a lower general price level than would be the case had the tax not been cut. This tax effect on the general price level is brought about through the mechanism of the tax shifting process. The shifting process not only diffuses the effects of a tax throughout the economy and shifts the tax to its effective incidence, but it is also the mechanism by which any change in the amount of tax is absorbed by an economy through a movement from one general price level to another.

To investigate the tax shifting process and its effect on prices, the following simplifying assumptions are made: a marginally balanced budget; a neutral monetary policy (in the sense of the supply of money being equal to and determined by the demand for money); the non-government sector's propensity to spend out of disposable income is equal to unity, that is, the non-government sector's propensity to save is equal always to its propensity to invest.

Let it be supposed that government increase the amount of income-effect taxation by the imposition of a withholding tax assessed on the gross pay of employees. The formal incidence of the additional amount of income-effect tax will not cause any change in the aggregate supply function. On the demand side the simplifying assumptions ensure also no change in the aggregate demand function. Increased government spending out of the additional tax revenue will be

51

expected fully to offset the reduced spending out of a smaller take-home pay. In a period short enough to exclude the possibility of retaliation by employees all that is likely to happen is some temporary disequilibrium while the economy adjusts to an increase in government spending relative to non-government spending.

Retaliation by Taxpayers

It is likely that an opportunity will arise, sooner or later, for employees to retaliate against the tax-imposed cut in their take-home pay by demanding from their employers an increase in gross pay. The evidence indicates that this opportunity will be taken by employees and that eventually employers will accede to these demands. Adam Smith concluded that all taxes imposed upon the gross pay of employees are shifted by employees onto their immediate employers.[1] He implied net of tax wage bargaining to be the general rule by arguing that a 20 per cent tax assessed on the pay of employees would result in a 25 per cent rise in their gross pay. Two hundred years later his view is supported by the results of statistical investigations using the extensive and detailed contemporary data now readily available.[2] The OECD reported in *Public Expenditure Trends* 1978 that 'labour unions do attempt to shift income tax increases forward onto higher money wages, and net of tax wage bargaining seems to be a rather common phenomenon in all OECD countries.' In the case of a withholding tax on gross pay the process of tax shifting begins with those pay increases that follow directly from employee retaliation against the tax increase. As employees recover from their employers the amount of take-home pay lost already to the withholding tax, the aggregate supply price rises by the full amount of the tax recovered. Moreover, with a progressive tax system higher gross pay is likely to lead to an additional tax liability as a result of some employees moving into a higher tax bracket, and this too will be taken into account in the pay negotiations. Thus an additional amount of income-effect taxation in the form of a withholding tax will cause, by its formal incidence, the retaliation which sets in motion a shifting of tax from employee to employer. This shifting process causes the value of Z to increase for all values of N by something probably in excess of the original amount of the additional tax. By assumption, the aggregate demand price is increasing simultaneously and equally with the aggregate supply price. The point of intersection is, therefore, rising vertically as illustrated earlier in Figure 5. Given the assumed conditions set out above (p. 51), the process of shifting the additional income-effect tax causes a rising general price level to be associated with an unchanged volume of output and employment. Although from a different cause, this situation is in appearance what Maynard Keynes called 'a state of true inflation'.[3] It is a state of 'inflation' also in the sense in which that term is used by Milton Friedman and others, as the money supply is increasing at a faster rate than the growth of real output.

As the general price level rises the purchasing power of all money incomes falls and it is in this way that the tax shifting process works to effect a diffusion of tax incidence throughout the economy. In the absence of complete money illusion, the erosion of real take-home pay by rising prices will be the cause of further pay demands by employees.[4] This is the phenomenon called 'the wage/price spiral', a label which tends to obscure the retaliation taking place on a much wider front. The pay of employees is not a special case, as the fall in the purchasing power of money affects everyone in receipt of a money income. Inevitably, for the same reason as employees, the receivers of money incomes other than take-home pay will be motivated, as soon as the opportunity arises for them, to retaliate against rising prices by seeking higher money incomes. With the advent of this second stage retaliation, an extensive self-generating element is injected into the process of tax shifting. As money incomes in general rise in an attempt to regain lost purchasing power, then further price rises follow and in turn are the cause of further retaliation by the receivers of money incomes and so on and so on. Progressive taxation adds to these inflationary pressures. Even assuming no increase in tax rates, there will arise automatically additional tax liability as a result of bracket creep. However, although the diffusion of tax incidence by rising prices injects an element of self-generation into the process of tax shifting, it does, at the same time, tend to bring about a running down of the process. As noted already, most economic theorists from Adam Smith to the present day conclude that those in receipt of certain classes of money incomes cannot retaliate against the incidence of any tax that happens to fall upon that income. As the tax incidence becomes more and more diffused throughout the economy, an increasing amount of tax will fall upon those who cannot retaliate by further shifting. Meanwhile the residual balance of the tax becomes so thinly spread that it is less and less likely to motivate those who are able to retaliate. The tax shifting process ceases when the formal incidence of the tax which caused the initial retaliation is diffused by the process of shifting into an effective incidence which cannot, or does not, motivate further shifting.

A cut in the amount of income-effect taxation will motivate a tax shifting process in the reverse direction to that which follows upon an increase. During the time this takes to work through the economic system the process will lead, given the assumptions set out above, to a fall in prices with little or no change in the volume of output and employment. For example, a reduction in the amount of withholding tax assessed on the gross pay of employees will result, through its formal incidence, in an increase in take-home pay by an amount equal to the tax cut. At the next round of pay negotiations net of tax wage bargaining is

likely to lead to a lower settlement than would otherwise
have been the case in the absence of a tax cut. Adam Smith's
argument and contemporary evidence suggests net of tax
wage bargaining works both ways. Thus some part, or even
the whole, of the benefit from the reduction in tax is shifted
from the employees to the employer in the form of lower
labour costs than otherwise would have been the case had
there been no tax cut. The working of market forces in a
trading economy will ensure that eventually firms reflect
their lower labour costs in the selling prices of their output.
As this latter stage becomes general the benefit of the tax cut
is spread throughout the economy.

The formal incidence of an increase in the amount of
supply-effect taxation, by definition, will cause an increase
in the value of Z for all values of N equal to the amount of the
additional tax. Simultaneously, given the assumptions specified (p.51), the value of D will increase for all values of N by
that same amount. Thus in this case the tax shifting process
may be considered as being activated automatically, as firms
have no option if they are to remain in business but to adjust
to the tax-imposed increase in their supply price. The formal
incidence of an increase in supply-effect taxation is, therefore, with the minimum of time lag, a direct cause of rising
prices and an erosion of real incomes. As the opportunity
arises it is to be expected that all income receivers will
retaliate against the erosion of their real income. In so doing
they motivate the second stage of the tax shifting process
which is indistinguishable from that following upon an
increase in the amount of income-effect taxation. Again,
once this second stage is set in motion it too will continue
until the formal incidence of the additional tax is diffused
throughout the economy into an effective incidence which
cannot, or does not, motivate further retaliation. That a
change in the amount of supply-effect tax tends automatically by its formal incidence to affect prices almost immediately is the reason why demand management techniques rely

on taxes of this class as so-called 'regulators'. Nonetheless, the demand management argument, that a change in the amount of supply-effect tax will cause only a once and for all change in prices, is valid only on the assumption of persistent and complete money illusion or in cases where the change in the amount of tax is so small that the resultant change in prices is too little to activate retaliation.

Tax Inflation

As has been argued, the tax shifting process is essentially a mechanism by which an economy adjusts to a change in the total amount of taxation through a movement from one relatively stable general price level to another relatively stable general price level. For this adjustment to be completed, with the minimum of interference to the volume of output and employment, a neutral monetary policy is necessary. For this reason periods during which tax shifting is proceeding may be appropriately described, depending on direction, as *tax inflation* or *tax deflation*. During a period of tax inflation a neutral monetary policy requires the monetary authorities to allow the rate of increase in the money supply to be in excess of the rate of growth of real output. This is because, at any given volume of output and employment, rising prices will lead to an increase in the demand for money. If during such a period the rate of increase in the money supply is restricted to the rate of growth of real output then inevitably output and employment also will be restricted. In a period of tax deflation the converse holds; in this case a neutral monetary policy implies a rate of increase in the money supply less than the rate of growth of real output.

Tax inflation describes the condition which prevails for as long as an economy is adjusting to an additional amount of total tax through a rising general price level and, therefore, at any given level of activity the demand for money tends to rise as prices rise. During a period of tax inflation a rate of increase in the money supply in excess of the rate of growth of real output is only the *proximate* cause of the rising prices. The *primal* cause of rising prices during the period is the additional amount of taxation. So long as the tax shifting process continues, an apparently lax monetary policy is not so much the cause of inflation as a policy necessary to minimise the effect of fiscal policy upon the level of activity. This does not deny Milton Friedman's assertion that 'inflation is always and everywhere a monetary phenomenon',[5] for undoubtably without the excess money supply the rate of inflation would be less and might even be a zero rate. Nonetheless, when applied to a period of tax inflation, Milton Friedman's assertion is likely to mislead for it refers to no more than a proximate cause of the rising prices. When an economy is going through a period of tax inflation, any attempt to 'squeeze inflation out of the system' by restricting the supply of money must also restrict output and employment, if not precipitate a slump. The concept of tax inflation is consistent also with the restated quantity theory of money, for it admits of a stable demand function for real balances, M/P. When fiscal policy generates forces tending to raise the value of P, then the value of M will need to be increased if a restrictive effect on the level of activity is to be avoided. However, the concept of tax inflation does deny Friedman's proposition that 'fiscal policy is unimportant for inflation'.[6] Fiscal policy is very important for inflation, for it is fiscal policy that is often the primal cause of rising prices, and it is the rising prices that lead to an increase in the money supply in excess of the rate of growth of real output.

The Economic Upper Limit to Taxation

The terms tax deflation and tax inflation describe conditions in an economy which can exist openly, given a neutral monetary policy, for only so long as it takes that economy to adjust to a change in the total amount of taxation through a movement from one relatively stable general price level to another relatively stable general price level. In the case of tax inflation this assumes the total amount of tax to be no larger than that which the process of tax shifting can diffuse into an effective incidence at some higher general price level. The larger the amount of taxation the longer the tax shifting process will continue and the higher will be the eventual general price level. Thus it is possible for the total amount of tax to be such as to cause the shifting process and the rise in prices to continue indefinitely. Tax inflation then becomes a persistent condition. For any economy, therefore, there must be, in given conditions, a maximum amount of total tax revenue which at some general level of prices is consistent with a zero rate of inflation without restricting the level of activity. This total amount of taxation is that amount which the shifting process can diffuse over a period of time into an effective incidence. Following the terminology of Colin Clark in his pioneering empirical studies[7], this amount of tax revenue relative to net national product (NNP) at market prices can be called the *economic upper limit to taxation*.

Provided that general government total tax revenue does not cause the economic upper limit to taxation to be exceeded, then tax inflation is a temporary condition limited to whatever period of time it takes the shifting process to diffuse the formal incidence of taxation into an effective incidence. When total general government tax revenue causes the economic upper limit to taxation to be exceeded, then there will exist a condition of persistent tax inflation. Whether persistent tax inflation is open or suppressed is determined by government policy. In fully controlled economies it is usually suppressed. In open trading economies, with relatively free markets faced with persistent tax inflation, however, it is government monetary policy that determines the trade-off between the rate of inflation and the restriction of output and employment. Demand management techniques may succeed in reducing the rate of inflation for a time, but in the longer-run can only make the situation more intractable. Increasing taxes in an attempt to dampen real demand raises prices and restricts the growth of NNP at market prices. The restriction of growth and the rising prices combine to reduce the economic upper limit to taxation and lead evenually to a state Milton Friedman describes as 'stagflation'. A tight monetary policy will suppress persistent tax inflation at the expense of a restriction on output and employment although, as in the case of the United Kingdom, this may be associated with improvements in productivity. However, irrespective of any short-run benefits, should the level of activity begin to recover then the rate of inflation will again start to accelerate. The improvement in the level of activity provides the conditions conducive for retaliation against taxation and so the process of tax shifting restarts. The only effective policy to eradicate persistent tax inflation is a policy of cutting tax revenue which is directed towards reducing firms' tax inflated costs and expanding NNP at market prices. When the economic upper limit to taxation is being exceeded, a prosperous economy and a zero rate of inflation are incompatable.

1. Adam Smith, *The Wealth of Nations*, BkV, Ch II, Part II, Art.III
2. Ronald Burgess, *Fanfare to Action*, Economic Study Association, 1973; Thomas Dernbury, *The Macroeconomic Implication of Wage Retaliation Against Higher Taxation*, International Monetary Fund Staff Papers, Nov. 1974; C.J. Bruce, 'The Wage Tax Spiral; Canada 1953-70', *Economic Journal*, 1975.
3. J. M. Keynes, *The General Theory of Employment Interest and Money*, p.303.
4. John Hicks, *Economic Perspectives – Further Essays on Money and Growth*, OUP, 1977, p.6
5. Milton Friedman, *The Counter-Revolution in Monetary Policy*, Institute of Economic Affairs, 1970.
6. Ibid., p.24.
7. Colin Clark, *Economic Journal*, 1945 & *Taxmanship*, Institute of Economic Affairs.

6
Tax and Unemployment

Any tax sooner or later inflates the aggregate supply price and, in an open trading economy the extent to which this causes firms to become uncompetitive, must lead to some unemployment. More importantly, in the conditions prevailing throughout the western industrialised economies, some methods of taxation operate directly not only to increase unemployment but also to destroy jobs permanently. To earn a living in a trading economy it is necessary to trade and to trade one must have something to sell. When, as is the general case in contemporary trading economies, those who supply the labour to productive enterprises have no title to the the resulting output, then they have nothing to sell but their labour. The complement to this is that those who expect to enjoy title to the output must buy in, along with everything else, the labour necessary to produce that output. Thus, in addition to markets for output, there arises a labour market in which the buyers and the sellers of labour come together and through the process of bargaining determine what is, in effect, a market price for labour. Given this condition, withholding taxes assessed on the gross pay of employees and payroll taxes imposed on employers combine to reduce directly the prospects for employment by distorting the labour market through the effect of these taxes on both the bargaining process and the market price for labour. In addition these forms of taxation directly destroy jobs by acting as a subsidy on what from the employers' point of view are labour-saving investments. In fact these kinds of investments are motivated by the employers' need to avoid tax in order to sustain competitiveness.

The Price of Labour

In economic theory the market price for labour is usually called 'wages', but this term is open to many conflicting interpretations. Professor A. W. Phillips, when formulating what has become known as the 'Phillips curve hypothesis', took money wages to be the market price for labour.[1] This view of wages was described by Milton Friedman as being 'utterly fallacious' and he called upon 'every economic theorist from Adam Smith to the present' in support of his contention that the market price for labour is 'real wages'.[2] In this instance Milton Friedman underrated Adam Smith's perspicacity. In *The Wealth of Nations* Adam Smith wrote: 'The money price of labour is necessarily regulated by two circumstances; the demand for labour, and the price of the necessaries and conveniences of life'.[3] He acknowledged also that this money price depended on an agreement between employer and employee 'whose interests are by no means the same'.

In the closing decade of the twentieth century Adam Smith's second circumstance refers to the purchasing power of take-home pay (gross pay including benefits in kind less withholding taxes) in terms of what, following Pigou, are called 'wage goods'. This aspect of pay is of little direct concern to employers but it is of direct concern to employees. It is a factor determining the bottom limit below which an employee, as a seller of labour, is not prepared to settle with an employer. As has been argued (p. 52) when the purchasing power of take-home pay is eroded by rising prices, it is employees who react. When the most employers are prepared to offer as take-home pay is less than the money sum represented by this bottom limit, employees withdraw from the market as suppliers of labour. Thus Adam Smith did not argue real wages to be the market price for labour, as Milton Friedman claimed and others often imply, but rather that real wages are only one of the factors determining the money price and the supply of labour.

The first circumstance noted by Adam Smith as regulating the market price for labour is determined today by the demand from firms for the labour supplied by employees. This demand for labour is a *derived* demand — a demand derived by firms from the demand for the outputs produced by that labour. Thus the demand for labour is determined not so much by conditions in the labour market as by conditions in the markets for outputs. These markets for outputs determine also the per-unit market prices of outputs. As a result, therefore, the most firms can afford to pay for the labour demanded is determined by the conditions in the markets for output rather than by labour market conditions. As the markets for outputs move in favour of the sellers of outputs (firms) then the demand for labour will tend to increase and the most firms can afford to pay for that labour will tend to rise. As the markets for outputs move in favour of the buyers of outputs then, the demand for labour will tend to contract and the most firms can afford to pay for the labour demanded will tend to fall. In the general case firms can effectively demand labour only to the extent that it is profitable for them to do so at the current market price they must pay out for labour.

Pay Bargaining

In the process of pay bargaining the top limit above which the price for labour cannot rise is set by the most firms can afford to pay for the labour they demand. The theory of Keynes leads to the conclusion that pay settlements tend towards this top limit rather than, as generations of economists and others have asserted or implied, the least employees are prepared to accept. According to Keynes' theory the take-home pay included in the aggregate supply price is an aggregate determined by the top limits set by firms in the process of pay bargaining. This is so by definition, for the take-home pay included within the aggregate supply price is, after allowing for expected total tax liability, the most firms can afford to pay directly to their employees consistent with the expectation of a minimum profit just sufficient to induce them to produce the output from an amount of labour represented by that take-home pay. If for some reason, other than a change in withholding tax, actual take-home pay turned out to be less than that expected by firms at any level of activity, then actual profit would exceed that amount of profit the expectation of which was just sufficient to induce firms to operate at that level of activity. In this event the competitive struggle would cause firms to revise their individual supply prices downwards consistent with a minimum profit after taking into account the lower market price for labour in terms of take-home pay. This revision would lead to a shift downwards of the aggregate supply price curve (Figure 1, p.24) and, assuming an unchanged demand price curve, the point of intersection would move to the right corresponding to a higher level of activity. This higher level of activity would be that at which firms expected the most they could afford to pay out as take-home pay would approximate to actual settlements. Conversely, if for some reason, other than a change in withholding tax, actual take-home pay settlements turned out to be more than firms expected at any given level of activity, then actual profit would be insufficient to induce firms to sustain that level of activity. The upward revision of their individual supply prices would lead to an upward shift of the aggregate supply price curve and, assuming an unchanged aggregate demand price curve, a contraction of activity. The lower level of activity would be again that at which firms expected the most they could afford to pay out as take-home pay for labour would approximate to actual settlements.

The assumption of an unchanged aggregate demand price does not invalidate the conclusion that take-home pay settlements tend towards the most employers can afford to pay, although it may exaggerate the resulting changes in the level of activity. When settlements turn out to be less than expected, then spending on consumption is likely to be less than expected. However, since the propensity to spend on consumption out of disposable income is generally less than unity, the shortfall in consumption demand is unlikely to be as great as the shortfall in take-home pay settlements. The propensity of government to spend out of tax revenue plus borrowing requirement is always (p.26) equal to unity, but spending on investment is more a matter of conjecture. Larger profits than expected will tend to increase investment spending while a shortfall in the expected spending on consumption will tend to contract investment spending. Taking all relevant factors into account it is to be expected that the downward shift of aggregate demand curve will be somewhat less than the downward shift of the aggregate supply curve. As a result of this the expansion of activity would be less than if the aggregate demand curve was unchanged. Nonetheless, the economy would still tend towards a level of activity at which expected take-home pay settlements and actual settlements were close to each other. Conversely, when actual take-home pay settlements turn out to be more than expected the aggregate demand price curve will shift upwards, but by something less than the aggregate supply price curve. The contraction of activity will be less than would be the case with an unchanged aggregate demand price curve but, again, the economy would tend towards a level of activity at which firms expected the most they can afford to pay out as take-home pay approximated to actual settlements.

It is implicit in Keynes' general theory of employment that pay settlements tend towards the most firms expect they will be able to afford to pay for the amount of labour being demanded. From an employer's point of view this 'most' refers to labour cost (inclusive of taxes on employment) rather than take-home pay, and this offers an explanation for the process of pay bargaining seeming not to operate in some, especially the non-unionised, sections of the labour market. It has become commonplace for firms to offer jobs at a certain stated gross pay (i.e. inclusive of withholding taxes), giving no bargaining position to a prospective employee other than taking or not taking the job. When the sum being offered is the most an employer expects to be able to afford to pay, there is no room for bargaining in an upwards direction, although if the offer is above the least an employee is prepared to accept then, in an effort to secure the job, the employee may offer to accept less. On the other side, when a prospective employer does not get any applicants, or suitable applicants, at the sum offered, the options are either to withdraw from the market or to find some means of improving the offer so as to attract those able to supply the labour required. Should there be a mass of suitable applicants, then the employer will either take care to select the employee who seems likely to give the most in return for the pay offered or withdraw temporarily from the market and re-advertise at a lower figure. In these cases it appears to the job applicant that the pay offered is a fixed price rather than a market price. Thus the revolutionary conclusion to be drawn from Keynes' theory, that pay settlements tend towards the most employers expect to be able to afford, admits to the possibility, from the point of view of an employee, that in some cases the pay bargaining process may be more covert than overt. This fact of experience is one the labour market has in common with many other markets — especially trade in western countries between retailers and final consumers.

The Pay Bargain Gap

In pay bargaining both sides expect to gain an advantage
from the eventual settlement, for, in common with other
bargaining, it is not a zero sum game. Thus for the pay
bargaining process to reach a negotiated agreed settlement,
there must exist a positive gap, *the pay bargain gap*, between
the most employers can afford to pay employees for the
labour demanded and the least employees, or prospective
employees, are prepared to accept in return for supplying
that labour. Given both a pay bargain gap and settlements
tending towards the most employers can afford to pay, then
actual settlements will be responsive, like other market
prices, to the general conditions in the markets for output,
and also will *appear* to be responsive to conditions in the
labour market. With a contraction in demand for outputs the
aggregate demand price curve will shift downwards, tending to reduce the demand for labour and the most employers
can afford to pay for that labour. In the labour market, an
increasing deficiency in demand for labour will be associated
with a fall in the average level of settlements, or at least
settlements will be lower than might otherwise have been
the case. As the average level of settlements falls the
competitive struggle between firms will drive employers to
revise their expectations in respect of labour costs in a way
tending to shift the aggregate supply price curve downwards. As this happens market forces begin to work towards
a slowing down and eventual reversal of the downswing in
activity. Conversely, with an upswing of activity following
upon an expansion of demand for outputs, market forces will
work towards a slowing down and eventual reversal of the
upswing. As the aggregate demand price curve shifts upwards with the upswing of activity then the demand for
labour by employers will expand and the most they can
afford to pay for that labour will rise. In these circumstances
the average level of pay settlements will rise, causing

employers to revise their expectations in respect of labour costs in a way tending to shift the aggregate supply price curve upwards.

Given circumstances that allow for both pay bargaining and the free play of market forces, then Keynes' general theory of employment supports the hypothesis of a Phillips curve relationship between the rate of change of pay settlements and the rate of unemployment. When an economy is on an upswing of activity the rate of unemployment will tend to fall and be associated with a tendency for pay settlements to rise. Conversely, when an economy is on a downswing a rising rate of unemployment will be associated with a tendency for pay settlements to fall. However, this conclusion appears to be inconsistent with Keynes' hypothesis of an economy being in stable equilibrium in slumpy conditions, as illustrated in Figure 1 (p.24), with 'involuntary unemployment' accounting for a significant mass of the unemployed. For Keynes' hypothesis to be sustained it needs to be shown that in certain cases the pay bargain gap ceases to exist, preventing the free play of market forces.

Maynard Keynes formulated his general theory of employment during the early 1930s, a period of world-wide depression following upon, particularly in the United Kingdom, a decade of persistent deflation. The domestic purchasing power of sterling rose by 60 per cent from 1920 to 1930, that is to say 12s/6d (62.5p) in 1930 was equal to the purchasing power of £1 in 1920. In combination, depression and deflation will cause the aggregate demand price curve to shift downwards substantially and relatively quickly and with this the most employers can afford to pay for labour will fall sharply. On the other side, the least employees are prepared to accept in return for supplying their labour is determined more by psychological forces than by market forces and as a consequence will respond only slowly to the changing economic conditions. Thus the pay bargain gap is closed, or may even become negative, and the least employees are prepared to accept becomes the determining factor for pay settlements. Once this has happened market forces will not work towards a recovery except in the very long run. This long run will last for as long as it takes economic and social conditions to break through the psychological barriers of employees and force down the least they are prepared to accept in return for supplying their labour to something less than employers can afford to pay. During the 1930s Keynes and others advised giving the economic system an external shock by increasing government expenditure on public works and encouraging a small rise in the general price level as a way out of that particular depression. Certainly it is arguable that such a policy might well have increased the most employers could afford to pay for labour relative to the least employees were prepared to accept. However, while this may offer an explanation and solution for the 1930s it does not apply to the present time. In the United Kingdom the domestic purchasing power of the pound sterling has been falling continously for over fifty years, and during the decade of the 1980s declined by over 40 per cent. For more than the past twenty years in the United Kingdom persistent inflation, as well as unemployment, has always been significant and sometimes very high indeed.

Taxes on Employment

An alternative explanation for the high rates of unemployment during the last quarter of the twentieth century is offered by the monetarist school of economic thought. A sharp fall in the rate of inflation, they argue, will affect immediately the most employers can afford to pay for labour, but on the employees' side inflationary expectations will adjust far more slowly. This circumstance may lead also to a closing of the pay bargain gap and cause employers to contract their demand for labour as the market price, determined by the least employees are prepared to accept, becomes more than employers can afford to pay. In this case the hump in unemployment will last as long as it takes employees to revise their inflationary expectations and stop holding out for substantial annual pay increases. This monetarist account does explain at least part of recent high levels of unemployment, but it does not explain a major part of the problem in countries such as the United Kingdom where unemployment has been on a rising trend since the mid-1950s. In cases such as these the major cause of unemployment is the persistent squeezing of the pay bargain gap by an increasing reliance by succeeding governments on the revenue from payroll and withholding taxes, assessed on the gross pay of employees. In combination these two methods of raising tax revenue are the most effective in destroying employment opportunities, and they may be accurately described, therefore, as *taxes on employment*.

The imposition of a payroll tax does not affect the most employers can afford to pay for labour in total, but it does reduce immediately, by the full amount of the tax, the most employers can afford as gross pay to their employees. In this way all payroll taxes act directly and immediately by their formal incidence to close the pay bargain gap. United Kingdom examples of this method of taxation are the former selective employment tax and national insurance surcharge and the current employers' national insurance contributions. Of greater importance in the longer run, is the fact that such payroll taxes act in a way to subsidise so-called 'labour-saving investment'. As this tax effect operates over the longer run, its results are far more difficult to correct. If an employer can replace an employee by a machine then the liability for payroll tax is avoided. In the multitude of marginal cases it is just this element of tax avoidance that makes the new labour-saving investment profitable. Once the investment has been made it will last for a long time and so set up a new pattern of production and trade. Thus to avoid tax, jobs are destroyed, perhaps for ever. Whether this new pattern is real progress or a distortion of the economy is a matter of chance. Much of this tax-induced labour-saving investment is not saving labour from the point of view of the community as a whole. Often the result is no more than a transfer from paid labour to unpaid labour.

For example, it was no accident that the move to self-service retailing in the United Kingdom coincided with the imposition of selective employment tax in 1966 by the then Labour Chancellor of the Exchequer. The new tax was intended to help expand employment in the manufacturing sector by increasing the cost of labour in the service sector. The intention of the administrators was in one part fulfilled. The new tax hit the multitude of small and family owned retailers hard and their trade was taken away by large groups with sufficient funds available to avoid the tax by investment in self-service stores. From the narrow point of view of the retail trade this investment was labour saving and brought about measurable improvements in productivity. From the point of view of householders it was quite the reverse. It ceased to be commonplace for a householder to place an order with a shopkeeper and have the goods delivered to the doorstep by a roundsman or errand boy. The tax priced the overwhelming majority of householders out of the market for such personal services. Today a householder has to get out the car, drive to the supermarket, have the hassle of finding a parking space, trudge round the supermarket and collect the goods needed from the shelves, queue at the checkout point, load the car, drive back and then unload the car — all very time-consuming unpaid hard labour. Did the enormous investment in response to the tax really save labour? Certainly the tax contracted the field open to profitable trade and in so doing destroyed paid jobs. Selective employment tax has long been abolished but the new pattern of retailing, having been set up, continues to grow apace. The old success story of errand boy to boss is a possibility no longer — taxation has knocked out the bottom rungs of the ladder. The possibility of a success story is replaced by the actuality of the young unemployed who, lacking work experience, are unable to get jobs.

As with payroll taxes so withholding taxes assessed on the gross pay of employees also close the pay bargain gap. The imposition of a withholding tax does not affect the least employees are prepared to accept as take-home pay, but by its formal incidence it does increase by the full amount of the tax the least employees are prepared to settle with an employer in terms of gross pay. As has been argued already (p.52), withholding taxes are shifted by employees onto their immediate employers and so eventually inflate the cost of labour to an employer. Through the tax shifting process this method of raising tax revenue, like payroll taxes, destroys jobs as the resulting high cost of labour encourages labour saving investment. Other deleterious effects include a tendency for employees to be less willing to supply additional labour when required. They prefer to spend their extra time in activities which do not attract tax. 'Why should I work for the taxman?' becomes the all too frequent response to an employer's request for overtime working. A flourishing black economy is the end result.

Taxes on employment (payroll and withholding taxes on gross pay combined) not only work directly to close the pay bargain gap and so make both pay negotiations more difficult and poor industrial relations more likely, they also destroy jobs, distort an economy, and, by encouraging the black economy, bring the law itself into disrepute. From time to time it is argued that the authorities should clamp down on the black economy as the revenue gained would enable some other tax rate (usually income tax is chosen) to be halved, or some such substantial reduction. This is nonsense. Given the continuation of employment taxes, if the black economy were to be brought within the tax net, there would be no net gain in revenue as the output it currently produces would cease to be produced. The economy as a whole would be that much the poorer. The black economy exists and thrives on tax evasion: at tax-inflated prices its effective demand would vanish. The first step towards eradicating the black economy can only be the removal of its major cause by the abolition of taxes on employment.

When taxes on employment are increased to a point where they close the pay bargain gap completely, then a fundamental change takes place in the operation of the labour market. The most employers can afford to pay for the labour they demand becomes, after allowing for employment tax liabilities, no more than the least employees are prepared to accept as take-home pay for supplying that labour. There is no room for bargaining. With this the labour market ceases to operate to bring buyers and sellers of labour together, so they may negotiate and agree a market price for labour advantageous to both parties. The market begins to operate as if it were a fixed price monopoly market. Since the least employees are prepared to accept as take-home pay is unresponsive to changes in market conditions, employers find themselves faced with a fixed price, or cost, for labour which is determined exogenously by government effectively at the time it legislates to fix the amount of taxes on employment.

When, by means of taxes on employment, governments close the pay bargain gap and create a fixed price labour market then both employees and employers find themselves in a take-it-or-leave-it situation. In this circumstance a kind of Phillips curve relationship continues to hold but, after allowing for changes in the purchasing power of money, the direction of causation from the standpoint of unemployment is reversed. The rate of unemployment ceases to be the independent variable and becomes the dependent variable. Instead of pay settlements appearing to respond to conditions in the labour market, as Professor Phillips hypothesised, it is the total amount of taxes on employment that determines conditions in the labour market. United Kingdom experience during the second half of this century shows that when employment taxes are increased then, 12 to 15 months later, the rate of unemployment begins to rise. On those fewer occasions when employment taxes have been truly cut, then, 12 to 15 months later, the rate of unemployment begins to fall. In the United Kingdom there have been times when some part of a temporary hump in the rate of unemployment may have resulted from a slowing down in the rate of inflation, but the major part always was, and continues to be, the direct result of tax policies pursued since World War II by successive governments at Westminster.

1. A. W. Phillips, 'The Relationship between Unemployment and the Rate of Change in Money Wage Rates in the United Kingdom, 1861-1957', *Economica*, Vol 25, pp.283-99.
2. Milton Friedman, *Unemployment versus Inflation*, Institute of Economic Affairs, 1975, p.15.
3. Adam Smith, *The Wealth of Nations*, Bk.I, Ch.VIII.

7
The Physiocratic Tradition

The Physiocrats thrived in France during the third quarter of the 18th century and founded what may be considered as the first school of economic thought, in the modern sense of that term. They called themselves 'économistes' and they acted as an organised group of thinkers who intended to influence the economic policy of their government. The name by which the school is known today is derived from a collection of writings by their master, Francois Quesnay, in a book published by Dupont de Nemours in 1767 entitled *Physiocratie, ou constitution naturelle du gouvernement le plus avantageux au genre humain*. The designation Physiocrats (Greek *physis*, nature, *kratein*, to rule) however did not become current until the 19th century and calls attention to the emphasis the school placed on natural laws and the natural order. The importance of the physiocratic school in the context of this work is that they advocated the abolition of taxation and its replacement with a natural source of public revenue. Further, they believed that government should confine its expenditure to a limit determined by the public revenue naturally available and not the complete reverse — the accepted wisdom today — which advocates expected public expenditure to determine the level of taxation.

Every productive process involves the consumption of some wealth in the production of new wealth and, as the Physiocrats recognised, the one ought to be deducted from the other in order to assess the difference. This difference measures the net increase of wealth which, since the time of the Physiocrats, has been known as the 'net product'. They argued, however, that only agricultural production had this unique power of yielding a 'net product'. Only when engaged in agriculture did a labourer reap more than he and his industry consumed throughout the year. Consequently commerce and manufacturing were classed as 'sterile'. Sterile did not signify that these occupations were useless but only that they were unproductive in the sense that no extra wealth was produced. They contributed nothing to the 'net product' as the wealth they consumed equalled the new wealth they produced. A great gap in the Physiocratic theory was that they had no concept of value added. Indeed value was rarely mentioned in their writings. Loaves of bread when exchanged for a ploughshare were considered to be of equal value. The largest part, if not the whole, of the 'net product' produced by agriculture accrued, it was argued, to the landed proprietors in the form of rent. On this conclusion regarding the circulation of wealth, which was compared in importance to the discovery of the circulation of blood in the history of biology, rests the Physiocrats' proposals for the 'Impôt Unique' or single tax.

Public revenue and the theory of taxation forms a large part of the Physiocratic system and is one of the most characteristic portions of their work. Today it is common to ascribe social problems to an unequal distribution of wealth, but the Physiocrats rightly emphasised the true source of injustice to be the burden of taxation. General taxation, they argued, was a deviation from the 'natural order' which must result also in a contraction of future output. After the landed proprietors have deducted the 'net product', there is left to agriculture only the wealth necessary to maintain output. Should the cultivators of the soil be burdened in addition with taxation then there will be that much less capital for the land and this must result in a smaller gross product the following year. They concluded that it is the landed proprietors who, one way or another, will eventually pay the

tax. Since commerce and industry produces no more than
the wealth they consume, the imposition of a tax burden on
them must reduce their consumption and limit their pur-
chases of raw materials. The only escape from a diminished
future production would be if the so-called 'sterile classes'
were able to raise their prices by the amount of the tax
burden. Again, one way or another, the tax would be borne
by the landed proprietors. Given their system, the only
available source of public revenue is the 'net product' and, to
conform with the 'natural order', this must be collected
from the landed proprietors. The essential distinction between taxation and the Physiocratic 'impôt unique' is that,
while taxation is of necessity arbitary, the 'impôt unique'
was regulated by a natural norm which gave the amount of
the 'net product'. They calculated that 30 per cent of the 'net
product' would be sufficient to cover public expenses and
Dupont de Nemours emphasised that, if this proved to be
insufficient, 'there is only one natural and reasonable conclusion to be drawn from this, namely, curtail the expenditure'.

Although the Physiocratic system has little in common
with, and is not directly applicable to, an advanced industrial
trading economy much of their work is of contemporary
interest. For example, their argument that taxation inevitably restricts future production or leads to an increase in
prices, and that there exists a natural source of public
revenue which in turn imposes a natural limit on government expenditure. The first is today a fact of common
experience and may be deduced from the theory of Keynes
formulated more than a century and a half later. The second
probably provides the only sure way of restraining spend-
thrift modern governments, by imposing upon them the
discipline of having to live within their income as do private
persons. Also of interest is their demonstration of the special
nature of the income from land and their proposal for a
single tax. This latter concept was expounded within the

context of an industrial trading economy, apparently without any prior knowledge of the earlier Physiocratic work, in the second half of the 19th century by the American, Henry George. George left behind him a worldwide single tax movement which continues today with centres in most countries and regular international conferences.

Henry George

Like the physiocrats Henry George stressed the natural order of things and was in addition, it is interesting to note, more concerned with the quality of life and the environment than most of the late 20th century 'Greens'. The idea that the environment is a common heritage for future generations was fundamental to his work. He is best known today for *Progress and Poverty*, first published in San Francisco in 1879. It remains an all-time best seller on the subject and was subtitled 'An enquiry into the cause of industrial depressions and of increase of want with increase of wealth . . . the remedy'. For George the remedy was simple and practical: 'abolish all taxation save that upon land values'.[1] Like all great works of political economy it was directed at a public issue of topical importance at the time of writing. An earlier example of this was Ricardo's formulation of the theory of rent which provided the theoretical support for his argument that the high price of corn was not caused by the high price of cornland, but on the contrary, that the then high price of cornland resulted from the high price of corn.[2] For Ricardo corn was a synonym for wheat and the prevailing high price of wheat was an important public issue in the United Kingdom at the beginning of the 19th century.

Similarly in the 20th century Keynes was writing for his time when he argued in his *General Theory* that supply could not be relied upon always to create its own demand.[3] During the inter-war years of the depression the continuing deficiency of aggregate effective demand was a public issue of international importance. Henry George was concerned to demonstrate that the growth of population, especially the growth of densely populated cities, is not of necessity associated with ever increasing poverty: an important public issue in his time which remains very much with us today. The pessimism of the then authoritative arguments based on the assumption of the niggardliness of nature was not for George. 'It is a well provisioned ship', he wrote, 'this on which we sail through space'.[4]

Although a contemporary of Alfred Marshall, Henry George remained a Ricardian. He considered that, for example, 'as to the law of rent there is no necessity for discussion'.[5] This did not prevent George from recognising that Ricardo's theory of rent failed to explain fully the rapid growth in the rent, or price, of land in a developing trading economy such as the United States in the late 19th century. He accepted the then orthodox view that the cause of the rapid rise in rent was increasing population, but concluded that Ricardo's explanation, the lowering of the margin of cultivation, was of minor importance. Of major importance, he concluded, was that increasing population brought out in land special capabilities otherwise latent, and attached special capabilities to particular lands.[6] The exposition by which he arrived at this non-Ricardian conclusion can shed much light on contemporary issues of public finance. George begins by supposing a first immigrant arriving in an unbounded savannah every part of which is equally fertile.[7] This supposition is of importance for George's argument for it precludes any possibility of rent arising in accordance with Ricardo's theory. An increasing population cannot be the cause of lowering the margin of cultivation in an unbounded savannah every part of which is of equal fertility. The first immigrant would settle, George supposed, somewhere by chance, but the subsequent immigrants would be attracted to the lands as near as possible to the first settlement. He observes with St Thomas Aquinas[8] that man is gregarious by nature, but carries the observation further. Not only would they do this in the expectation of enjoying a better quality of life from social intercourse, but also in the expectation of enjoying material gains as a result of one settler co-operating with his neighbours on particular tasks. As the new settlement grew, George noted, there would very soon arrive a specialist blacksmith, a wheelwright, a store, and so on. For reasons of business these specialists would be attracted to central locations. Every settler would gain an advantage from having these services provided locally, but the first immigrant, being handily located at the centre already, would gain more than those later immigrants located at the periphery, which by this time might be relatively far off. As George put it, land at the centre of the settlement 'begins to develop a productiveness of a higher kind'.[9] Thus the value of the first immigrant's land will begin to increase relative to that of later immigrants, not from any lowering of the margin, but from the margin of production being raised. This increase in value George called 'rent'. As the population grows the process continues and the settlement becomes a village, the village a town and perhaps eventually a great city. The farmers, argued George, may move on but the specialists must remain at the centre of exchanges to be viable. Eventually the land of the first immigrant, now being located at the centre of a thriving community, becomes so valuable as to enable him to lease or sell his land and retire as a very rich man. As rents and the price of land increase so the proportion of the wealth produced going to capital and labour diminishes — hence George's title, *Progress and Poverty*.

Mindful of the important social and political issues of his day, Henry George emphasises in his savannah story the association of increases in population with the growth of the income he called rent and the consequent extremes of wealth and poverty. But an association, however well proven, does not imply causation in either direction. The demonstration that it is only after the population has grown to a certain size that the price of land is greatly enhanced, is not sufficient grounds for concluding that the population growth is the cause of the enhanced price or is dependent solely upon this growth.

Today George's story is instructive more for what he failed to observe than for what he actually observed. For example, the story begins with a settlement of neighbourly self-sufficient farming households co-operating one with another, but trading only what happened to be surplus to their household requirements. With the arrival of the black-smith and other specialists a fundamental change takes place. A settlement of self-sufficient farming households is changed into a *trading* economy. The various individual enterprises no longer produce an output primarily for their own sub-sistence but in part, and in certain cases wholly, for the purposes of trade. George takes no account of this funda-mental change. Again, George, like Ricardo, fails to observe the necessity of an *effective demand*. What causes the black-smith and other specialists to set up in the new settlement is not the population size, but the existence of an effective demand for their services and products at least sufficient to yield them a living. Size and density of population may be a rough indicator of the existence of an effective demand for certain services, but the one is not of necessity positively linked to the other. More important is that, even given the initial effective demand, an embryonic trading community will not grow automatically into a town or a great city as George supposed. If trade and industry are to flourish within a community, then certain expenses must be incurred to provide the *public services* required by those living and working at particular locations. The development of the 'higher kind of productiveness', as Henry George called the manifestation of locational advantages, will not persist if Main Street is allowed to remain a lawless quagmire and the whole area bereft of all public services. Indeed, in such conditions, the locational advantages of operating at the centre or any other part of the community might disappear completely, with trade and industry departing for other centres where public expense is incurred for the provision of necessary public services. The population would follow jobs. George failed to note that the rise in the price of land at those sites enjoying locational advantages is in fact a measure of the effective demand for public services. Although he recognised that in the circumstances he supposed, the rise in the price of land had nothing to do with the productiveness of the soil, the dictates of Ricardian economics obscured from him the actual cause and led him to conclude the rise to be a different mode of Ricardian rent manifested when increasing population brought out other natural gifts otherwise latent in the land.

1. Henry George, *Progress and Poverty*, Bk.VIII Ch.II.
2. David Ricardo, *The Principles of Political Economy and Taxation*, Ch.II.
3. J.M. Keynes, *The General Theory of Employment, Interest and Money*, Ch.II.
4. Henry George, *Progress and Poverty*, Bk. IV Ch. II.
5. *Ibid.* Bk.III, Ch.II.
6. *Ibid.* Bk.IV Ch.II.
7. *Ibid.* Bk.IV Ch.II.
8. Thomas Aquinas, *On Princely Government*, Bk.I, Ch.II.
9. Henry George, *op. cit.* Bk.IV, Ch.II.

8
Neo-Classical Arguments

The imposition of taxation ensures that a community as a whole is forced to pay for whatever public goods and services its government in its wisdom may decide to provide. At the macroeconomic level it may be argued that taxation is a justifiable imposition. At the microeconomic level, however, the sum exacted from the individual taxpayer is unrelated to the public benefits received by that taxpayer. Thus, given the principle of private property, taxation can be justified only as a macroeconomic solution to the need for public revenue. It lacks microeconomic foundations: an individual taxpayer does not receive the public benefits paid for through taxation by that individual. The basis of the argument in favour of redistributive taxation is that it ensures some members of the community pay more while others pay less or nothing for public benefits. Redistributive taxation is a crude attempt to rectify the distribution of wealth that results inevitably from government's failure to conform to the principle of private property. Results cannot be mitigated while causes are allowed to remain.

Reality is obscured further by the operation of a tax system which is intended, in accordance with the 'ability to pay principle', to introduce a measure of so-called 'fairness' between individual taxpayers. Within the limits of practicality governments try to establish a positive relationship between the amount of taxation exacted from an individual taxpayer or corporate body and their pre-tax net private income. Such good intentions of governments are thwarted at the outset. It is apparent that individually taxpayers are not amenable to the imposition of taxation; all react to the impact of a tax and where possible shift the incidence (Chapter 5); some take steps to avoid the tax legally while others attempt illegal evasion. A primal cause of the so-called 'black economy' is the reaction of individuals to taxation. Yet the imposition of taxation is now universal and, lacking knowledge of any alternative source of public revenue, is accepted by taxpayers as a necessary evil. The macroeconomic solution of funding public spending out of tax revenue is accepted by the contemporary economic orthodoxy as a self-evident truth. The possibility of an alternative solution has vanished from orthodox economic thought and its literature.

The Macroeconomic Case

The macroeconomic solution to the question of public finance was put explicitly by Enrico Barone writing during the early part of this century.[1] First, he defined what he called 'public needs' as being whatever a government happened to provide 'in any country at any time'. Thus according to his definition the extent and content of 'public needs' is not determined necessarily by economic factors; in certain countries at certain times the determining factor might be, for example, the prevailing political ideology. Barone then proceeded to distinguish two categegories of 'public needs' which he defined as 'those which are, and those which are not, susceptible to individual and specific demand and divisible supply'.

'Public needs' of Barone's first category being 'those which are susceptible to individual and specific demand and divisible supply' are not, he argued, of necessity to be supplied by government for they can be supplied by the private sector at 'economic prices'. An economic price, according to Barone, may be an open market price or a monopoly price or a price agreed in some other way. In today's terms 'economic prices', however agreed, may be taken to be current selling prices at a level a producer expects will yield a net income sufficient to cover the full supply price including a minimum profit. While Barone accepted that goods and services included within his first category of 'public needs' could be provided by private enterprise, he admitted that some might with advantage be supplied by government.

The second category of 'public needs' which Barone defined as being 'those which are not susceptable to individual and specific demand and divisible supply' may be interpreted as covering those goods and services which Adam Smith referred to to as the 'necessary expenses of government'. Such goods and services are necessary for the efficient working of a trading economy but, as Barone highlights, it would seem that the ordinary mechanisms of the market cannot automatically translate this 'public need' into an effective demand to which private sector firms can respond. From the view of a private sector producer not only is the supply indivisible but there is no indentifiable buyer with whom a bargain may be struck in the expectation of covering the full supply price, including a minimum profit. In these cases, Barone stated, government initiative is required. If government is to take this initiative then clearly it must command a sufficient public revenue to cover the necessary expense involved.

To Barone, as with most other writers on public finance, public revenue meant tax revenue. Following the orthodox line he assumed the imposition of taxation to be justified by economic necessity. As it is impossible by his definition to finance the second category of 'public needs' by individual pricing ('economic prices'), then they must be financed by taxation ('political prices'). To provide for the second category of 'public needs' he asserted that government have no alternative but by means of taxation to distribute coercively the total cost throughout the community according to an individual's income. On this assertion of 'no alternative' rests the macroeconomic case for the imposition of taxation.

Barone went on to assert that 'private persons do not demand public goods' — an assertion that does not follow from his definitions. There may be no 'individual and specific demand' for armed nuclear submarines, but this is not to say that collectively private persons do not demand such weapons as a way of providing the community with an adequate means of defence. This assertion led him to argue that the size of the supply of public goods is determined by a majority making decisions through some form of voting. In turn, the size of the supply of public goods and services decided upon by a majority vote determines the amount of tax to be imposed and distributed between taxpayers 'according to established principles'. This line of reasoning led Barone to conclude that ultimately the size of what today is called the public sector is determined by the majority, only within the limits set by the amount of taxation individual taxpayers are prepared to accept as tolerable. More recently Professor Prest writing on the same subject echoed Barone by stating, 'the very bareness of the economic principles set forth will make it clear that we are on the borderland where economic and political considerations meet and mingle inextricably with one another'.[2] This 'bareness of economic principles', Professor Prest concluded, leads modern economists to seek a political solution by devising appropriate principles of voting. Thus, by assuming public revenue is always and inevitably tax revenue, writers on public finance have been led to pose questions that their science is not equipped to answer.

Although the drift of Barone's arguments has led economists into realms outside the scope of economic analysis, this should not be allowed to obscure his significant contribution to the understanding of public finance. Arguing exclusively from economic grounds, he shows that the private sector and market forces cannot provide in every case all that is necessary for the efficient working of a trading economy. If the goods and services included within his second category of 'public needs' are to be provided, then government initiative is necessary. By isolating on the basis of economic criteria a category of 'public needs' that can be provided only as a result of government initiative, Barone comes up against the question of public revenue. He answers this question with an unsubstantiated assumption which orthodox economics accepts as a self-evident truth. Drop the assumption and one is led to a clear statement of the important issue to be investigated: How is government to command the public revenue required to fund these necessary initiatives?

Writing a little earlier than Barone, the French economist Paul Leroy-Beaulieu also argued that there are 'many cases where private initiative cannot take the place of governments'.[3] He used this argument not only to justify taxation as being necessary, but also as an argument against the reduction of taxes in certain circumstances. 'Let no one say', he wrote, 'that citizens would take care of these matters if government, instead of imposing excess taxation upon them, left them with the money of which this excess taxation deprives them.' From this statement Leroy-Beaulieu may seem to be heralding the post World War II demand-side school, but it has to be remembered that he considered a tax take in excess of 12 per cent of private incomes to be exorbitant. Nonetheless his view is topical to the extent that it conflicts with the policy prescriptions of the now dominant supply-side school. Supply-siders would seem to have reverted for inspiration to the 'golden maxim' of Jean-Baptiste Say, 'the very best of all taxes is that which is least in amount': a maxim of immediate appeal to taxpayers and therefore to politicians in their attempts to attract votes.

The Railway Example

By way of an example of the necessity for government initiative, Leroy-Beaulieu took the then topical case of a new branch railway which exerts a beneficial influence over a very wide area. The difficulty facing a privately-owned railway company is, he pointed out, that many of the beneficiaries from the enterprise will not use the railway and so will not contribute to its supply price. Some traders will use the branch line to carry their goods to other less congested markets and so will contribute through the cost of carriage. The net financial benefit they receive is measured by the higher selling prices obtained less the cost of carriage to the new market. Other traders, however, would continue to use their local market which, being less congested than before the new branch line was constructed, would be also now yielding better prices. For these traders the gross financial benefits bestowed by the branch railway accrue as a free gift from the owners of the line. 'This is why', concluded Leroy-Beaulieu, 'many public works cannot be carried out for private account; they would ruin private entrepreneurs, while being highly remunerative for society as a whole'. However, in the tradition of orthodox economics, he used the argument that private enterprise cannot in every case replace government enterprise to support the imposition of taxation. He did not consider the possibility of an alternative source of public revenue that in practice would charge all the beneficiaries the current market price for the financial benefits each received from the very existence of the branch line, apart from whether any particular individual beneficiary actually used the branch line or not.

The example of a new branch railway used by Leroy-Beaulieu provides a better illustration, and is brought into sharper focus when a distinction is made between the fixed or capital costs of constructing and maintaining a railway

forced to pay in excess for external economies (public benefits) which may or may not be available or required by them, while to others they accrue as a free gift. These circumstances must result in an ever increasing maldistribution of income and wealth within that community, plus all the distortions, injustices and tensions concommitant with such a condition. In certain cases the market, unaided, cannot ensure that the private sector provides all the goods and services necessary for the efficient working of a trading economy. Nonetheless, to rely on tax revenue as a source of finance in those cases requiring government initiative, multiplies the problems to be resolved.

The market is a distinguishing characteristic of a trading economy and the basic mechanism of a market is the process of bargaining. Trade may flow between countries, markets may be international, but the process of bargaining takes place between an individual buyer and an individual seller. The outcome of the bargaining process determines the market price. When there appears to be no individual buyer with a specific demand and when the supply is indivisible, then a direct process of bargaining is precluded and the market cannot give the necessary price signals to producers in the ordinary way. When this applies to goods and/or services necessary for the efficient working of a trading economy, then public initiative must act in place of private initiative. It is self-evident that as private initiative incurs a private expense to be met out of private income, so public initiative incurs a public expense to be met out of public revenue. Thus far Barone, Leroy-Beaulieu and other writers at the turn of the century made the case clearly and contributed much to the advancement of public finance theory. However, they assumed that the expenses of public initiatives leave government with no alternative but to impose taxation. This assumption obscured their contributions. As later writers on public finance have taken their assumption as an axiom, the issue remains unresolved.

Alfred Marshall's Contribution

In his major work *Principles of Economics* Alfred Marshall did not treat issues relating to public finance as a separate subject for discussion. Local rates are given an appendix to themselves (appendix G) but, while taxes are considered in a number of places, it is mostly by way of illustrating the particular subject matter being investigated. This has tended to obscure Marshall's most important contribution to the understanding of public finance and contributed to it being ignored by later specialist writers. In chapters X and XI of Book V, in particular, he provides evidence of a link between public outlay and effort and the current market price of land. These two chapters shed much light in those cases which Barone argued, for example, needed 'public initiative' charged at a 'political price'. Marshall argues that public work and outlay creates external economies which become manifested in the enhanced value of land.

In two chapters on marginal costs[4] Marshall, by implication, rejects the applicability of the Ricardian theory of rent for determining the market price of land in a trading economy. He argues that in a trading economy what makes land in general rich or valuable is determined by the extent of the opportunities which the occupation of a given site is expected to grant to its occupier for the time being. When dealing with agricultural land,[5] Marshall states these external economies to be largely the 'product of growing *public* prosperity' (italics in the original). This led him to distinguish between the 'private value' and the 'public value' of land. What he calls 'private value' is that part of the net annual value of land which is the result of the landowner's and/or occupiers work and outlay. The net annual value of land after the deduction of 'private value' he calls 'public value'. Thus, according to Marshall, the annual value of land, 'private value' plus 'public value', is produced wholly or largely by human work and outlays and, therefore, cannot be determined by the Ricardian theory of the rent of land. (In the Ricardian sense 'rent' arises from 'the original and indestructible powers of the soil'[6] and that, which is both original and indestructible, cannot be produced by human endeavour.) However, having distinguished between the 'public value' and 'private value' of land, Marshall did not use his newly defined terms exclusively. He went on to state that the 'annual value of land' could be called 'true rent', so obfuscating the issue by reintroducing Ricardian associations.

It would seem that Marshall himself was confused by the Ricardian associations of the term 'true rent' when considering the effects of 'a special tax on the annual public value of land'.[7] He argued that the 'special tax' levied on 'true rent' would deter landowners from making outlays to improve the methods of cultivating their land, which developed the latent resources of the soil in the expectation of a net return in excess of normal profits. The excess return would be, concluded Marshall, a 'true rent' and subject therefore to the 'special tax'. While a return on the latent resources of the soil might be classed as a 'rent' in the Ricardian sense, it cannot form part of the 'annual public value' or 'true rent' as defined by Marshall. The excess returns expected by the landowner are the direct result of an outlay by that landowner on improvements in the methods of cultivating his land. That these improved methods developed the latent resources of the soil is immaterial. Thus, according to Marshall's first definitions, the supposed outlays cannot increase the 'annual public value of land' but only its 'private value'. This being so the expected excess return over normal profits would not be subject to the 'special tax'. In fact the outcome is likely to be precisely opposite to that forecast by Marshall. A 'special tax' when levied on the 'annual public value of land' will encourage rather than deter landowners to make outlays on direct improvements to their land. For a time the innovator, having a monopoly of the improvement, would expect to enjoy as a private income a net return on the outlay in excess of normal profits. This provides the carrot for such innovation. Market forces would provide a stick for competitors. They would be driven to follow suit or risk becoming uncompetitive and, as a result, lose market share, or even go out of business. As the improvement became general usage then competition in a free market would erode the excess net return and, in the longer run, lead to the benefits flowing to consumers in the form of lower prices, or better quality, or some combination of the two.

In the chapter on 'marginal costs in relation to urban values'[8] Marshall provides further evidence of a link between public effort and outlay and the current market price of land. Unfortunately he again obfuscates his contribution by multiplying terms. He uses the term 'situation value' to cover the money value of the net advantage, enjoyed by the occupier of a particular site, resulting from the external economies and diseconomies created by the 'general progress of the industrial environment'. The extra annual income that can be earned by the occupier of land having a 'situation value' he called 'situation rent'. The 'situation value' of a particular site to any industry, including agriculture, is, he argued, the excess money value of the site over its 'agricultural value'. The 'agricultural value' of land he took as being the value of the free gifts of nature to be enjoyed by the occupier of that land. This led Marshall to define 'aggregate site value' as 'situation value' plus 'agricultural value'. He took 'aggregate site value' to be the current market price of land after allowing for any direct improvements made on that land — in the case of building land the current market price of a cleared site. That the greater part of 'situation value' is 'public value' Marshall considered to be obvious, although his various definitions and multiplicity of terms caused him to admit to a number of exceptional cases. The exceptional cases arise where 'situation value' has been produced by private outlay and effort and is, therefore, to be considered as 'private value'.

When dealing with the exceptional cases of 'situation value', Alfred Marshall, like Leroy-Beaulieu, also considered the effects of contructing a new railway, at the time very much a topical issue. Marshall's purpose was not related to public finance but to whether any resulting increase in 'situation value' should be classed as private profit or 'public value'. He argued that when a group of landowners used their own combined funds to finance the construction of a new railway which was not expected to yield any great return directly, then any income from the increase in the value of their lands should be regarded as private profit — an exceptional case where an increase in 'situation value' enhanced 'private value' and not the 'public value' of land. From this example he concluded that all cases where the owners of land invested their capital, not in direct improvements to their land, but to fund enterprises which they expected would make external economies available to the occupiers of their land and thereby increase its value, should be regarded as exceptional.

What Marshall did not consider was the case of an owner of land within the catchment area of a new railway, or similar enterprise, who decides not to contribute funds to that enterprise. Economic forces cannot discriminate between the land owned by a contributor of funds to some new enterprise and the land owned by a non-contributor of funds. If the values of some parcels of land falling within the influence of a new enterprise are affected, then the values of all parcels of land within that sphere will be affected — an aspect of indivisible supply determining Barone's second category of 'public needs'. Thus, in the case of a non-contributing landowner the increase in the value of his land, resulting from the availability of external economies created by some new enterprise, must accrue to that landowner, not as profits on capital invested or 'private value', but as a free gift from those who have invested their capital in the new enterprise — as 'public value' not 'private value'. As Marshall did not consider the case of non-contributors, he did not consider, as did Leroy-Beaulieu, the possibility of such enterprises, although advantageous to the community as a whole, proving ruinous to private entrepreneurs due to their inability to charge all those benefitting from their outlay and enterprise. Had he considered all the possibilities, he may have seen the need to redefine 'public value' and 'private value' relative to what he now called 'situation value' of land, thereby contributing even more to the advancement of economic science.

In the same chapter Marshall wrote, 'any increase in the net income derived from the free gifts of nature which was not brought about by, and did not supply the direct motive to, any special outlay on the part of the landowners is to be regarded as rent for all purposes'.[9] Again Marshall confuses the issue by substituting terms with Ricardian associations; but even so this qualification does not cover the case of the non-contributing landowner mentioned above. The non-contributing landowner is the recipient of an increase in net income derived, not from a free gift of nature, but from a free gift of external economies made available by the work and outlay of other members of the community. What Marshall had stated in the preceeding chapter is applicable to the immediate issue. 'Barren heath land', he wrote, 'may suddenly acquire a high value from the growth of an industrial population near it: though its owners have left it untouched as it was made by nature'.[10] In this instance he stated explicitly that this increase in the value of land is produced by 'the actions of men, though not of its individual owners'. Since this value of land is produced by the actions of men it cannot give rise to a 'rent' in the Ricardian sense and so Marshall classed it as 'public value'. From the barren heath land example it must follow that any increase in the value of land, resulting from some enterprise to which the owner of that land is a non-contributor of funds, must be classed as 'public value'.

From the aspect of public finance Marshall's work on marginal value is confusing and tends to obscure his important contribution to the subject. Nonetheless, he does show that in those cases where, apparently, supply is indivisible, the money value of that supply, or its supply price, is manifested in the enhanced value of land. This comes about as the actual supply produces external economies, or benefits, to the occupiers for the time being of particular sites. In the first instance these accrue to the occupier for the time being as a free gift, but, given private property rights over land, upon the sale of those rights or the renegotiation of the rent the money value of the advantages pass to the landowner. Thus the second category of Enrico Barone's 'public needs' which he stated as being 'not susceptible to individual and specific demand' is shown by Marshall to be susceptible, albeit in a roundabout way. At the time a particular site is sold or the rent renegotiated, there is an individual seller and the otherwise indivisible supply is, in effect, divided. At the same time there is an individual buyer, purchaser or tenant, with a specific demand for the advantages that accrue to an occupier of that particular site. These two parties, the buyer and the seller, or landlord and tenant, in the normal way strike a bargain which determines its current market price. At this price both parties to the bargain expect to gain an advantage. Marshall's contribution thus advances the work of Henry George and, in terms of neo-classical economics, shows how market forces operate to cause the value of public work and outlay to be reflected in the current market price of land.

1. Enrico Barone, *Giornale degli Economisti*, April/May 1912.
2. A.R. Prest, *Public Finance*, 1960.
3. Paul Leroy-Beaulieu, *Traite de la science des finances*, Vol.II, Bk.II, 1906.
4. Alfred Marshall, *Principles of Economics*, Bk.V, Ch.X & XI.
5. *Ibid.*, Bk.V, Ch.X.
6. David Ricardo, *The Principles of Political Economy*, Ch. II.
7. Alfred Marshall, *Principles of Economics*, BkV, X, 4.
8. *Ibid.*, Bk.V, XI.
9. *Ibid.*, Bk.V, X, 1.
10. *Ibid.*, Bk.V, X, 4.

9
Public Revenue

As argued explicitly by the Physiocrats and Henry George, and as may be deduced from the works of Alfred Marshall and others, the price of land is the key for collecting public revenue as an alternative to an arbitary levy such as taxation. What appears to be the market price of land is in fact a measure of the market price of those goods and services which Barone defined as being 'not susceptable to individual and specific demand and divisible supply'.[1] In common usage it is usual to refer to owners of land, or landowners, but the Law of England, for example, provides more precise terminology. What is owned is not the land as such but freehold property rights over land. Those persons who are commonly referred to as landowners are in practice freeholders, for what they own are the freehold property rights over land. The current market price of these rights over land is the sum of two distinct parts which may be called, following Marshall's argument, their private value and their public value. Marshall's definition of private value proved to be too wide and this led him into difficulties when, in his next chapter, he came to define 'situation value'. Given vacant possession, the private value of a freehold is that part of its market price a willing buyer will pay a willing seller for all the improvements resulting from the work and outlay *directly* on that land by the succession of freeholders and/or occupiers of that land. These improvements are properly called private value as first, in the nature of things, they ultimately fall into the possession of the freeholder for the time being. Second, the enjoyment of this property right by the freeholder conforms to the principle of private property (p.12). By definition, either the private value has been produced by the present freeholder's work and outlay, or, in the absence of evidence to the contrary, it is to be presumed the freeholder has received it by way of gift or fair exchange from those who did produce it. Any income yielded by private value, either in cash or kind, is a private income. It is a private income since it is the return on the freeholder's investment of work and outlay directly on the land over which freehold property rights are enjoyed. Where the investment has been made by an occupier who is not the freeholder then, depending on the terms of the tenancy agreement, the return may be the private income of that occupier until such times as a new bargain is struck.

The presumption of title to private value in favour of the freeholder may be objected to on the grounds, as Mill argued,[2] that the ownership of land does not of itself conform to the principle of private property. The substance of his argument is that no person can show they produced land itself or provide evidence that they received it by way of gift or fair exchange from whoever did produce it. Even if the validity of this argument is accepted, the objection does not hold in the present context. The private value of freeholds is produced over the years by the work and outlay of private persons or corporate bodies; titles pass in good faith from seller to buyer through to the freeholder who for the time being enjoys possession. The fact that in times long past freehold titles may have been obtained by conquest or fraud is immaterial. While the acquisition may have been wrong, the revival of a claim long dormant will cause a further wrong and for this reason most countries impose a legal time limitation. On these grounds it is equitable to presume that in the absence of recent evidence to the contrary, the present freeholder has title to the private value attached to the land over which the freehold property rights are enjoyed. The same presumption applies to any income that may be generated by private value. In conformity with the principle of private property a government has no right to impose a tax on the private value of a freehold or otherwise appropriate any part of it by force or fraud. Indeed a government has a duty to uphold and secure to private persons and corporations the full enjoyment of the private value of their freeholds. This duty applies with equal force to any income generated by the private value of a freehold for this is a private income. To enforce the payment of a tax on private value or private income as if it were a debt is to obscure the nature of the original wrong.

The public value of freehold property rights over land is that part of its current market price a willing buyer is prepared to pay a willing seller for the net *external* economies, advantages and other benefits an occupier expects to gain from the occupation and use of that land. Thus, this definition of public value is precisely what Marshall called 'situation value' and follows by contrast from the insertion of the term 'directly' when defining private value above. Alternatively, public value is the market price of a freehold less its private value. It is the actions of the community as a whole and, in particular, the provision of public goods and services by public authorities that produces the public value of a freehold. In a developing country an embryonic trading centre may grow to become an important city where, as Henry George argued and experience confirms, property rights over land change hands for astronomical sums of money. This will happen only providing the necessary public expenditure is incurred on such things as metalled roads, sewerage, drainage, water supplies, street lighting, law and order and so on. Should this necessary public expenditure not be forthcoming then the embryonic trading centre will atrophy by reasons of mud, disease and lawlessness. The high prices paid today for sites in major cities reflect their high public value produced largely at public expense. An example of how this manifests was featured in *The Times* (October 7th 1986). The article listed Aylesbury Grammar School, a free state school, among the top twenty boys' schools in England and noted 'House prices in the area pushed up as a result of parents moving into orbit'. The enhanced house prices are in fact a measure of the increased public value produced by this quality state grammar school within its catchment area. There is a specific demand for good education and in the market place most parents who can afford to do so are prepared to pay the price. Today some of these parents pay the price as fees to independent schools, while others pay for good 'free' state education through enhanced house prices. In cases like these, law and fiscal policy allows the increased public value to accrue to the seller of the freehold as if it were a private value.

The British government has announced that the capital and environmental costs of constructing the high speed rail link between the Channel Tunnel and the North is to be passed on to the users of that rail link. The rail link is forecast also to raise property prices significantly throughout its catchment area. By treating public value as if it were private value, the government will force users of the rail link, through higher charges, to make a free gift of windfall profits to the fortunate existing freeholders. This policy must result in higher charges and a lower demand for the service to the detriment of the community as a whole.

Both the private value and the public value of a freehold are produced over time by the work and outlay of people and, like all products, may be destroyed. Thus as neither value is 'original and indestructable' they cannot give rise to a rent in the strict Ricardian sense of that term. However, both values may give rise to a rent in the modern economic sense of a surplus over and above transfer earnings of a factor of production which is, during a given time period, in fixed supply. Both the improvements which give rise to private value and the externalities which give rise to public value take time to produce and during this time they may be considered as in fixed supply. Those enjoying already existing improvements and those occupying locations benefitting from already existing externalities during the limited production period may receive a rent in the sense of an income in excess of the transfer earnings of the particular factor in fixed supply. Again, both the private value and the public value of a freehold may give rise to a rent in the common usage of that term as a hire charge. For example, a regular payment (hire charge) for the flow of benefits and advantages expected to be received, including the additional income expected to be earned from the occupation of a particular site having a certain public value, may be called a rent. However, in economics the usage of the term rent in the context of the private and public value of freehold property rights over land is likely to be confusing if not misleading. Alfred Marshall is one example of being led into error by the Ricardian associations of the term rent. As has been argued, the income generated by private value is a private income, the regular payment a willing buyer may be expected to pay a willing seller for enjoying, through the occupation of a particular site, the various economic externalities reckoned as public value is rightly a *public revenue*. This description conforms to the principle of private property. Public value is produced by the public in general and by their public authorities in particular and so the income generated by these actions is a public revenue. Government has a *duty* to the public to collect this revenue on their behalf.

The Question of Land

No amount of work or outlay will produce land and, therefore, land of itself cannot have a private or a public value. Both these values are produced by the actions of people. Land falls into that category Marshall calls 'free gifts of nature' and, providing government performs its public duty by collecting public revenue, *land is a free good*. It may be argued that in the case of reclamation schemes land is produced, but this argument ignores the fact that the land was already there. The work and outlay put into reclamation schemes does no more than transform land covered by seawater into dry land. Depending on circumstances, the freehold property rights over this dry land may have a private value, a public value, or a combination of both. Again, the sun, sand and beauty of Spain's Mediterranean coast has existed for thousands of years, yet for most of that time the region was impoverished and property rights over land worth little or nothing. The relatively high prices of these property rights today is not nature's free gift to the owners of those rights, but a gift from those whose work and outlay has contributed to the prosperity of Northern Europe, to advances in transportation, to the building of roads, airports and the provision of all kinds of public services. It is all this work and outlay that has produced both the public value and the effective demand by giving to many thousands of people the opportunity of enjoying a Mediterranean holiday. The increase in public value makes it profitable to increase private values and it is these two combined that has greatly enhanced the prices of property in most parts of the region.

Land is different from natural resources. Although there are similarities, the differences between the two are of importance. Both land and natural resources are produced, so far as their physical composition is concerned, by nature without human effort and remain in their natural place in the universe, but there the similarity ends. To be classified as a natural resource the location of that resource must be known and, although it may remain for the present unused in its natural place in the universe as a reserve, there must exist, or be expected to exist, an effective demand. For example, there does exist today an effective demand for oil and thus known oil reserves are natural resources. In former times crude oil oozing to the surface resulted in what in the United States were called 'bad lands'. There was no effective demand for the crude oil and its presence on the surface rendered the land useless for agriculture. The inventions of more recent times have created an effective demand for crude oil and these former 'bad lands' gave access to an oil-field. Property rights over 'bad lands' became so valuable that the owners found themselves to be millionaires without any work or outlay on their part. Again, a distinction is required between natural resources and raw materials. For example, coal reserves lying unused in their natural place in the universe are a natural resource, but to a miner working at the coal face they are his raw material.

From Alfred Marshall's argument in respect of barren heath land,[3] it is to be concluded that natural resources give rise to a public value and, therefore, providing government perform their duty of collecting the public revenue, the necessary work of exploration is a matter for government initiative. This does not imply the need to expand the public sector by setting up vast state corporations, for in most cases there are likely to be advantages in government employing private specialist firms on the basis of competitive tendering. The United Kingdom has moved already some way towards the recognition of natural resources as public assets to be excluded from private property rights over land. It is not now possible for a freeholder in the U.K. to become an oil millionaire by fortunate accident, as freehold property rights do not extend to any oil that may found below the surface. The private sector firms that engage in oil explora-tion operate today under government licence. The impor-tant difference between land and natural resources is that human work and outlay cannot produce land, while natural resources are the product of the human work and outlay put into enterprises that lead to their discovery so as to meet an effective demand.

The Public Sector

Enrico Barone (p. 83) and most other writers on public finance assume the extent of the public sector to be determined by political rather than economic considerations. Orthodox economic theory reinforces this assumption by 'the very bareness of the economic principles'[4] it is able to provide. In practice governments decide on what is to be included or excluded from the public sector on a majority vote based largely on political expediency or ideology. The possibility of Alfred Marshall contributing to the issue was lost in a welter of exceptions to his definition of 'situation value' that followed inevitably from his definition of 'private value'.[5] For example, as mentioned earlier, while admitting that the larger part of 'situation value' is 'public value', he was forced to argue that, when the owners of freeholds invest their capital not directly on their freehold but in building a railway or some similar enterprise which gives to their freehold a 'situation value', then that value is a 'private value'. The income generated is to be considered, he concludes, as a private profit on their investment. This line of argument does not elucidate any economic principle but merely accords with current practice. However, when the private value of freehold rights over land are defined as above, so that public value is precisely Marshall's 'situation value', there emerges the possibility of determining the extent of the public sector by economic principle rather than political considerations.

Let it be supposed that government performs its public duty and collects the total public revenue for the purpose of defraying public expenses and there is no taxation. Given this circumstance, then the exceptional cases noted by Marshall where 'private value' is part of 'situation value' will not arise. Freeholders will be encouraged to invest directly on improvements to their freeholds to the extent that this is expected to yield a private income or benefit they consider to be an acceptable return on their investment. Such investment will enhance the private value of their freehold and may also enhance public values. For example, when two or three properties in a run-down street are improved then not only will the private value of those particular properties be increased, but the investment is likely to have an incidental effect of raising the public value of all properties in the street. However, apart from acts of philanthropy, freeholders and others will not be prepared to invest in enterprises that are expected to enhance the public values of freeholds rather than their private values. In such cases investors will know in advance that they cannot expect a sufficient return on their investment to make the enterprise a commercially viable proposition. The government will be collecting as public revenue that part of the income generated by 'situation value', which Marshall argued should be considered as private profit, so as to provide a sufficient return on capital outlay. In the supposed circumstance Marshall's exceptional cases illustrate an economic principle for determining the parameters of the public sector. Acting on this principle then, the public sector would cease to consist of whatever a legistlature by a majority vote may in its wisdom decide, as Barone accepted and contemporary governments act upon as if it were a self-evident truth.

Providing governments collect the whole of public revenue and do not appropriate by taxation or similar means any part of private income, then they may safely leave to market forces and private sector initiative all enterprises where the work and outlay is expected to yield a private value or income sufficient to cover the total supply price including a minimum margin of profit. The public sector may then be limited to the supply of those goods and services for which there is an effective demand by the community as a whole, but where also the work and outlay is not expected to yield a private value or income sufficient to provide an acceptable return to private investors. If such an effective

demand is to be met then, as Barone argued, public initiative
using public funds is necessary. When government act in
accordance with this economic principle their decision
making is assisted by a kind of built-in cost-benefit analysis
which determines whether there exists in reality an effective
demand and its extent. When the demand by the community
as a whole for government to supply certain goods, services
or benefits out of public funds is effective, then the meeting
of this demand will increase public value and the expected
revenue to a level that will cover the full supply price, or
that part of it which it would be self-defeating to attempt to
cover by receipts from market prices in the ordinary way. In
those cases where it is agreed the public value and expected
public revenue would not be increased to cover the expected
supply price, then there does not exist within the community
an effective demand sufficient to necessitate a government
initiative. Thus, with taxation abolished and given prudent
government, public revenue will be, by definition, sufficient
to cover all necessary public expenses. There will be room in
addition for limited public initiatives using public funds to
meet demands on political grounds, although they may not
be expected to be effective demands relative to any likely
increase in public value or revenue.

As noted above some public value and revenue is produced
by the general public automatically in pursuit of their
private ends at no public expense. Further, it is reliance on
taxation as a source of public revenue to defray public
expenses that has allowed government to escape from financial restraints and establish, as an accepted principle of
public finance, that they adjust their spending estimates to
the available public revenue. When government perform
their public duty of collecting the public revenue and act in
accordance with economic principle they become subject to
the same financial discipline as applies to the private sector.
Under these conditions, taking one year with another,
government is required to adjust its spending to expected

public revenue and this provides the much needed barrier to public profligacy.

1. Enrico Barone, *Giornale degli Economisti*, April/May 1912.
2. John Stuart Mill, *Principles of Political Economy*, Bk.II, Ch.II.
3. Alfred Marshall, *Principles of Economics*, Bk.V, Ch.X, para 5.
4. A.R. Prest, *Public Finance*, page 65.
5. Alfred Marshall, *Principles of Economics*, Bk.V, Ch.XI.

10

Towards Reform

Policy objectives such as a zero rate of inflation coupled with low unemployment, extensive social welfare, and economic prosperity require high levels of public spending. When that spending is to be funded by equally high levels of taxation or borrowing, a zero rate of inflation is incompatible with the other policy objectives with which it is coupled. The politicians may win votes by their promises, but upon election to government they will be unable to deliver in full. As has been deduced from the theory of Keynes and the work of Colin Clark, the imposition of any amount of taxation inevitably raises prices and also distorts and restricts production. When the amount of taxation exceeds a certain proportion of NNP at market prices, a government is confronted with a choice: a zero rate of inflation together with a persistent slump, or, persistent inflation and what may be passed off for a time as economic prosperity. The case argued in this work, the abolition of all taxation and its replacement by the collection of public revenue by government as a public duty, is a *prerequisite* for solving the major social and economic problems, including inflation and unemployment, that today appear endemic in industrialised trading economies. Only when this fundamental change in public finance is completed will social justice together with a stable general price level and economic prosperity become possible to achieve. Setting in motion the change is not an immediate panacea, although when implemented in an appropropriate way, it will bring forth immediate benefits.

109

The fundamental reform of public finance will take time to complete and the method by which it can be accomplished will vary from country to country, depending upon their particular circumstances. The first step in the process must be the production of a full valuation of current public value together with the required administrative arrangements for keeping the list of data up-to-date, preferably on an annual basis. This is not a difficult task and in the opinion of professional assessors would be much simpler than the re-valuations for the former local rating system in England and Wales. In 1963 The Rating and Valuation Association carried through their pilot survey of Whitstable U.D.C. area within nine months. Although carried out for the purpose of supporting an alternative proposal for local taxation, this survey in fact provided an estimate of public value as defined in this work. Following the publication of the public valuation lists further time, say up to a year, must be allowed for the hearing and settlement of likely objections. Thus experience suggests that in the United Kingdom the House of Commons would be able to determine a national rate and begin collecting some part of the public revenue within three years from a Bill first being introduced.

Upon the first assessment of public value, the public revenue that could be obtained from this source would be significant but no more than a proportion of the present total tax revenue. For the United Kingdom the pilot survey carried out by the Rating and Valuation Association implies that the first valuation could produce a public revenue in the same order of magnitude as local taxes. Nonetheless United Kingdom evidence shows conclusively that over a period of time there is a negative relationship between the proportion of NNP at market prices appropriated as tax revenue and the proportion accruing as net disposable property income.[1] As the tax proportion rises or falls inversely, then over time the proportion accruing as net disposable property income falls or rises equally. Income generated by public value is a significant part of what can be isolated from the standard national accounting system only as net disposable property income. Thus, as taxation is cut, public value will rise at the next revaluation and, with this rise, public revenue will increase, given a constant rate, and so allow a further cut in taxation. Having made the first step of collecting the public revenue directly available and reducing taxation by an equal amount, a government must wait upon the economy adapting to the new set of circumstances. Once the process of fundamental change in the method of public finance has been started a government may continue the process in the economy's own good time until all taxation is abolished and the full public revenue is being collected.

Any cut in the amount of taxation will result eventually in a rise of public value. However, it is important for government to select the taxes to be cut, whether national or local, that will affect directly the immediate benefits required by the economy. In the United Kingdom, for example, abolishing the employers' contributions to social security taxes (a form of payroll tax) as a top priority will tend to reduce unemployment quickly, as it would immediately reduce labour costs to all employers of labour. Such a move would not only reduce public expenditure by reducing claims on social security benefits but, by reducing labour costs, automatically improve the competitive position of home producers as against overseas producers and thus assist in rectifying an adverse balance of payments position. If, on the other hand, it was considered most desirable to expand consumer demand, then cutting the amount of taxation by raising income tax thresholds would be appropriate. This would immediately increase the amount of money in the pockets of those consumers who may be expected to spend a major part of an increased personal income. This again would create opportunities for cutting public expenditure since, as the number of income tax payers are reduced, the

work load of the Inland Revenue would fall. For the effi-
cacious continuation of change in the method of public
finance, it is essential that, when cutting the amount of
taxation, a government creates opportunities for reducing
public expenditure as well as achieving their short-run
objective. For instance, giving priority to reducing the
standard rate of U.K. income tax from 25 to 20 per cent may
be most desirable from the point of view of taxpayers and
may even marginally expand consumer demand but it will
not create opportunities for the government to reduce public
expenditure.

At a time when environmental considerations are para-
mount, the proposed fundamental change in the method of
public finance is of particular importance. By collecting
public revenue in place of tax revenue, a government will be
able to remove the causes of much environmental despolia-
tion rather than attempting to mitigate the results. Pollution
will continue so long as it is profitable and will cease when it
ceases to be profitable. Punitive taxation may be a possible
means of ensuring unprofitability, but at a cost to the
economy as a whole which is likely to prove unacceptable.
What may be profitable to the pollutor is, to everyone
suffering from the pollution, an external diseconomy which
will depress public value and so reduce the public revenue
available for collection by government. If it were known
that as a matter of practice a government would automatically make good the loss of public revenue from the pollutor,
then the processes causing polution would become unprofit-
able and cease. For example, should a river become polluted
with excess nitrogen, the public value of a water company's
rights of extraction would fall and with it the public
revenue. Providing farmers were aware that any loss of
public revenue from such a cause would be charged to them,
they would cease to apply excess nitrogenous fertilisers as
the net additional produce obtained would become loss
making rather than profit making. In the new circumstances

this method of removing the causes of pollution becomes capable of wide application.

The public revenue to be collected by government as a public duty is not an arbitary levy and is not, therefore, taxation in economic terminology (p.39). Public revenue will enter into the supply price of individual firms but unlike tax revenue it will not aggregate to inflate the aggregate supply price. By collecting the public revenue government will be charging occupiers the current market price for the publicly produced externalities available to them at the place they occupy. For productive enterprises it means that firms will be required to pay for the publicly produced externalities as they already pay for other services and raw materials consumed in the process of production: both sets of payments will cancel out upon aggregation. A difference between the two sets of payments is that public revenue will be charged not on the basis of what is *consumed* in the process of production but on the publicly produced externalities *available* to the site they occupy. This fact will both ease planning procedures and provide environmental benefits. Profitability will demand that firms seek to locate on those sites at which the publicly produced externalities available are those they need to produce competitively. At any other location they will incur unnecessary costs either as a result of paying a public revenue for externalities they do not require or by paying privately for externalities required but not available at the site they occupy. The tendency towards micro-dispersion (urban sprawl) will be replaced by a tendency towards micro-concentration as a matter of private choice without government compulsion.

The momentum of the process of change from tax revenue to public revenue will depend on government not attempting to increase its total income by niggardly tax cuts. When taxation is abolished, however, the public revenue to be collected will exceed the public expenditure needed by a prudent government for public services of all kinds. This will arise in the nature of things, for much public value is produced by the general public automatically at no public expense. For example, sites adjacent to a railway station enjoy an enhanced public value produced by the passing trade available from the number of passengers using that railway station. The enhancement of these public values incurs no additional public expense. The old private railway companies were well aware of this bonus and usually purchased the freeholds of adjacent sites before building the station. The excess of public revenue over necessary public expenditure sets a financial limit for social welfare schemes undertaken by government which are not expected to yield a public revenue sufficient to cover the public expense.

The challenge of our time is to awake to the possibility of taking steps towards realising the given right of humanity to a truly just society in which they may live and, as free individuals, live more fully. This awakening requires a lead from economics for it is largely market forces generated by economic ignorance that holds the world's population in thraldom. Economists must direct their work so that by its results they are recognised as 'trustees of the possibility of civilisation'. This requires them to observe the nature of present day trading societies and on the basis of these observations offer to governments and electors policy prescriptions in line with the aim of their science and indeed all sciences — that people may live and live more fully. Politicians also have their part to play as servants to the community. They must cease to pick and choose advice depending on their momentary political beliefs and what they hope to be to their political advantage while side-stepping discussion of alternatives or even pretending ignorance of such alternatives. Political democracy rests on politicians listening to the people in a free, full and honest discussion of all relevant alternatives in the light of current knowledge. The arguments in this work are put forward to assist such a discussion.

1. Ronald Burgess, *Fanfare To Action*, Ch.VII, Economic Study Association, 1973.

Index